WILL YOU CARE IF I DIE?

NICOLAS LUNABBA

WILL YOU
CARE IF I DIE?

Translated from the Swedish by Henning Koch

PICADOR

First published 2024 by Picador
an imprint of Pan Macmillan
The Smithson, 6 Briset Street, London EC1M 5NR
EU representative: Macmillan Publishers Ireland Ltd, 1st Floor,
The Liffey Trust Centre, 117–126 Sheriff Street Upper,
Dublin 1, D01 YC43
Associated companies throughout the world
www.panmacmillan.com

ISBN 978-1-0350-2257-1 HB
ISBN 978-1-0350-2258-8 TPB

Originally published in Swedish in 2022 as *Blir du ledsen om jag dör?* by Natur und Kultur.

The sources on pages 321–22 constitute an extension of this copyright page.

All photographs courtesy of Nicolas Lunabba.

1 3 5 7 9 8 6 4 2

A CIP catalogue record for this book is available from the British Library.

Typeset in Garamond Premier Pro by Palimpsest Book Production Ltd, Falkirk, Stirlingshire
Printed and bound by CPI Group (UK) Ltd, Croydon, CR0 4YY

Visit **www.picador.com** to read more about all our books
and to buy them. You will also find features, author interviews and
news of any author events, and you can sign up for e-newsletters
so that you're always first to hear about our new releases.

Will You Care If I Die? is an autobiographical story.
In order to protect those involved, the author has chosen to
change certain names, places and course of events.

For Elijah

1

You moved in today.

Your bags are piled up in the hall and you're sleeping on the couch in your training gear. Where you'll sleep after this, I don't know. Either I'll bring down the mattress from the attic or you'll have to stay on the couch.

I don't want you here.

I'm afraid you'll come to see who I am. That you'll find out about my personality traits or things that happened in my family in the past, which you'll dislike.

I'm afraid you'll grow too close to me. That you'll become demanding and suffocating in that way of yours I've come to know. I'm afraid that those nocturnal hours of total solitude, which I need so desperately, will be taken from me and that this will lead to anger and hatred and the ending of our relationship.

I don't trust myself. It worries me that you do. I'm afraid I won't be able to control the anger within me if you trigger it, and that I'll turn violent. That everything will go to hell.

When you came here a few hours ago I met you with an embrace in the hall. I asked you how your day had been, listened to your expositions, and retreated to the bedroom with the excuse that I was tired. I tried to be cool and distant, verging on terse. But you, usually so sensitive to the slightest change in my mood, didn't notice. You smiled broadly and looked around. Didn't understand you weren't welcome.

For a long while you rummaged around in the apartment. You looked for food in the fridge and the larder, without success. You went into the living room and sat down at the computer, then you passed out on the sofa.

That's when I got up. Stole in to have a look at you. At the sight of your sleeping body, I felt a chill of horror. How would this look in other people's eyes? What normal, rationally thinking grown-up human invites the children of strangers into his home? And lets them stay there? Stay the night? Move in?

Nicolas, what's really your intention here? Why do you spend your time with other people's children? What loathsome urge draws you to the boy?

Why not just notify the social services instead if you believe the boy is at risk?

I hear the voices in my head. I will them to come, in order to be filled with such self-loathing that I am able to distance myself from you and tell you to move back home.

I'm sitting on the bed now, with the computer on my lap.

There's a compact darkness outside the window. The street light sways back and forth at eye level, stencilling a cone of light in the pitch black, and the snowflakes ignite like fireflies as they whirl into the orange glow.

All else is still.

I hear the swish of ventilation and water pipes. I hear my neighbour's steps across the parquet flooring overhead. A moment ago, he pissed into the toilet, the purling sound forcing its way down with an unpleasant clarity. If I concentrate, I can also catch an intimation of the dull thumping of my own pulse. I hear the thumping against my temple. As if the heart has taken the place of the brain.

2

For many years now I have been working with young people in the areas that are described as 'vulnerable'. The children there seek me out. It's a talent of mine. I play basketball with them, I provide them with food, we study and hang out. The youngsters pine to be close to me and under my protection. I embrace them. I ruffle their hair. And I think about how they may die.

Twenty-two children and adolescents in close proximity to me have either been murdered, have murdered or have died from overdoses.

I can see their faces, their way of looking up at me, their eyes filled with curiosity and anxiety. And then, when death comes along or when a child kills, the way the light in their eyes is extinguished.

I have more difficulty remembering the children's funerals. I can only grab on to the odd fragmented memory. A small coffin, proportioned to the body. A worn-out football in a pile of flowers. A framed class photograph. The deafening silence. There's often a strange stillness at young people's funerals. It's as if those who are close to them are holding their breath. Until the silence is cut by the cry of a parent, like a bolt of lightning. A cry so heart-rending, so filled with despair, that the chilling realization of what has been lost also seems to strike me down.

There are far more children who survive than there are children who die. But most of them are walking into a future that will break them down, crush their dreams and ambitions, their sense of self, and their bodies.

I see it happening. I know what I can do to avert the tragedy, but I make an active decision to keep out of it.

Time and time again, I enter into close relationships with these children. I win their trust and respect; make them believe I'm a person they can count on, turn to, someone who sees them and cares. I pump them full of strength and self-confidence. I tell them that they have to stand strong. In this country they're nothing but *blattes* – anyone with an immigrant background – and the system is rigged against them, but they have the power within themselves to break free. I tell them that another future is possible. That everything can be changed, *they* can change, there's no need for them to live like rats for the rest of their lives. They are beautiful and important just as they are.

But because these kids are so ruined by the circumstances that shape them, the violence all around them, and because I never have the intention to actually do what needs to be done, which is to *fully take them on*, this raising of hope is only a way of drawing out the catastrophe, a prolonged deception. For a long time I used to declare to others, and to myself, the Swedish sickness of considering it abnormal, unseemly, indecent, and maybe even paedophilic to feel a sense of responsibility for – an emotional engagement with – other people's children. I rehearsed various retorts about how the asocial nature of the Swede impacted on young people in general, and *blatte* kids in particular. I offloaded this critique as often as I got the chance.

The problem – it pains me intensely to admit it – was that the only sort of pedagogic approach that seemed ethically defensible, and had some real effect, demanded emotional sensitivity, care and openness to the child. I could never live up to that.

I can't be that person I so desperately needed when I was a child, the one who wouldn't leave me alone with my haunted thoughts and feelings, the one who saw me.

I am past thirty years of age. I live in a small, two-room apartment on Möllevången in Malmö. I don't have one serious romantic relationship behind me, and the prospect of such a thing happening in the future isn't exactly looking bright. I hardly have any family. I see my older brother sporadically. I have an aunt in Ängelholm, a grandfather in a care home. No one else.

I'm a frightened human being. I've always felt tiny and weak, ever since I was very young. That is why I live the way I do.

I only enter into relationships with people who can't hurt me. I'm calculating: how involved can I get, how much can I allow myself to feel, without starting to love someone? That is how I stay on my feet.

Besides, I am saturated with violence. Few things have been so constant in my life as violence. I've sat astride another human being and, in a mad rage, beat them over and over, listening to their panicked yells slowly diminishing, with a feeling that I could keep hitting them until there's nothing left but a dark stain beneath me on the asphalt. That feeling, of utterly smashing another living human being. And the reverse: the total loss of control over my body. The feeling of someone wishing to destroy me. To this day I scan other men around me on the basis of the violence they harbour inside.

My father disappeared from my life when I was four. I have few memories of him. But those that I have are memories of violence.

The violence has grown inside me. I have a tendency to revert to it if I feel sufficiently cornered. A few years ago, while I was working at a primary school, I got so enraged with a boy called Hassan that once, in a blind fury, I grabbed him by the scruff of his neck and thumped him down on the floor. I held him down with my entire body weight and yelled directly into his face: 'You do not fuck with me! You do not fuck with me!' while punching my fist into the floor next to his head.

On the outside I do what I can not to reveal my vulnerability, my fear. I try to present myself as emotionally secure and controlled, rational and self-confident, a charismatic and intelligent man. This is a character – or a caricature – that I know you very much admire. My own – and, come to think of it, also your – ideal of masculinity is not only based on the maintenance of a facade. It also requires one to be the least needy party in all relations. The one that stays in control.

That must be the reason why I work with vulnerable children. Their eyes seek me out and, when I look into them, I know that I am someone.

On one hand, the work is important. A large number of people's lives have been made better by me. On the other hand, my motives are murkier. I'm not afraid of the ghetto kids. They don't scare me with their hard attitudes, their unyielding manner. That's why we click. That's why they soften and their defences come down and I can embrace them as they are. I get so much, I give so little. The kids would never accuse me of abandoning them. Even though I see them, and their acute need of love and closeness. They have no expectations of the world around them. Their self-esteem is so low that they blame themselves even when other people misbehave. In this sense, these children are easy to deal with. Small gestures of tenderness and appreciation are enough. Really one only has to avoid acting like an arsehole or approaching them with suspicion; this keeps them going for a long time. They want nothing more than to throw themselves into my arms. They do their utmost not to seem as if they are hanging on, or needy, or weak.

Some of the kids are so hardened that one hardly notices their inner chaos, and it takes a long time before their damage can be seen with full clarity. Others are less skilled. They flatter and talk in a grown-up way, they joke and laugh and do their utmost to be seen. Others are defiant and disrespectful, aggressive, seeking self-affirmation with every step they take.

The kids orient themselves to their fear of having their inferiority confirmed, as well as their fear of losing what little power and position they have. That's also one of the reasons why they kill one another. Which is why trivialities such as rumours, the coins in your pocket and taking offence can lead to murder. In actual fact, they're not so trivial. Things that other people might find too ludicrous to mention can be the last few pieces of wreckage that these drowning kids are clutching on to to stop themselves sinking to the bottom. They can convince themselves that the lie is true, that the worthless thing they have is precious, that they are the rulers of matters that are out of their hands and cannot be changed.

These children own nothing. They are disoriented and defensive, pendulously moving between self-loathing and forced feelings of bravado.

When I compliment them, they react as if they have been slapped – turning away in shock and shame. These children group themselves and enter into friendships in which the concept of loyalty is as strong as their fear of one another. They only have each other, unlike privileged children who have a number of social contexts to move between, spaces where they can experience security and a sense of belonging, where their personal integrity is not under threat. Where the interplay is not defined by a constant positioning and dominance. Where violence and the threat of violence are not forcing their bodies into passivity. And above all, spaces in which they have affirmation and love. At home, in school, in the sports club, the youth centre, their circle of friends, the neighbours, grandparents – and further, in the public space:

9

the supermarket, the swimming pool, the park, the cinema or library. If a conflict arises, or for some other reason they can no longer occupy one of these spaces, the loss and dissolution is much less painful since they have other spaces to be a part of.

What most characterizes a child at risk is the absolute opposite of this. He or she only has access to and feels secure – or at least less threatened – in a small number of spaces, which for this reason also take on a disproportionate value. The realization that one can lose one's inclusion, and what this loss would mean, is constantly on their mind. The sense of need becomes excessive. And for the same reason, people are willing to drag each other down to the bottom if anyone so much as hints at a desire to be a part of other fellowships, other spaces. Which is why children who have been friends, fighting together in a war against the whole world, can suddenly turn their guns on each other.

That's where I come in.

I see myself in them. But unlike the children, I am not lost in that feeling. I have learned to control it, in the same way as with time and effort one can learn to rein in a wild animal. I am no longer the same as these children, no longer constantly on my guard. The lack of equity in the relationship means that I rarely have to think of my own need for recognition or closeness. The children feed me. Hardly a day goes by without their letting me know how heavy I am, how wise and elevated. And I use this against them.

I know what to say and do to make them fall into line

with my dictates. Sometimes I hear them talking about me when they don't think I'm listening. Nick is cool, they say. He's not like the others. He cares for real. And I do. I care about the kids, I want their best. But I care about myself more, want more of the best for myself.

In certain cases, once I have spent a long time with one and the same child, maybe several years, and we have got to know each other deeply, I can almost say that I love them. That's how it is with you, Elijah. Because you're my kid. You're my boy. But I am also my kid, my boy. I feel sick at the thought that something could happen to you, that you could no longer exist. And I do my utmost to get you to seek out new ways and values in life, to create the strength in yourself to break free, abandon your existence at rock bottom, grow wings, rise up to the light. But there are limits. Those limits present themselves once the price for your well-being, your freedom, commits violence against how I wish to live my own life. And this is the basis for our interaction. That's how it looks, our unspoken agreement, which you accept and adjust yourself to. I'm the one who decides, and I'll find ways of retreating from relationships that I have come to see as damaging.

Put simply, one could say that I am exploiting my position in the age hierarchy. All children are controlled. All children have the power of adults inscribed onto their bodies. This is the very first form of oppression. Children know what's expected of them, how they're supposed to behave and express themselves, think and feel. They know what is of value, what lacks value, what will happen if they break against

11

the rules and norms that adults have heaped on them, and what the likely consequences will be. Bellowing voices, sharp eyes, raised fists, backs turned on them. Being ignored, humiliated, stepped on and abused. Adults have the power to cast children into a hell of shame and loneliness, and children know this well. This does not only apply to children in vulnerable situations. Whereas children in decent circumstances realize to a certain extent that their subjugation and exposure is temporary and that in due course, as they become adults themselves, they'll assume the same position and also hold power, the submission of vulnerable kids is existential. It's a part of their being. It will never go away.

3

The first time you and I saw each other I was standing on a stage during a basketball event at the Malmö Festival. It was just before midnight. I gazed out across the area and through the throng of people I saw a little boy making his way along.

There must have been a thousand people in motion in the park, and the reason why you in particular caught my attention was your loutishness. You shoved your way forward using your elbows, stuck your chin into the air and yelled in a high-pitched voice at people, telling them to get out of the way. You seemed either unafraid or so afraid that you had to play tough. Even though you were a full head shorter than the older boys sitting on the temporary stands, smoking, you challenged them to basketball matches. You had totally misjudged your position as an eight-year-old among teenagers.

I made my way down from the stage, tapped you on the shoulder, and asked if you wanted a game. You did, and while you were wriggling out of your jacket and putting down your bag, you looked me up and down. I asked people to give us some space, we played a game, and I won by seven points to nil. You started griping: 'One more time. Come on, man, let's play one more time!'

'We can have another game in a minute,' I said. 'But first I want to eat. Winning has made me hungry.'

I convinced you to come with me to the hot dog stand. I bought us both burgers and fizzy drinks, and we went down to the canal and sat on some steps. Music, laughter and yells from the fairground and the basketball court thundered against our backs. The starry sky reflected in the black smooth water at our feet. Your cockiness was as if blown away; you went for your food and avoided my glance.

Once your timidity and hunger had lessened, and you picked up the courage to look at me, you started talking. About what a crap school you went to, who your favourite players were, and your dream of playing in the NBA. We sat there until long after the event was over, and then you wobbled off on your oversized bicycle. You had found a person to cling to. And ever since that night, that's precisely what you've done. Clung on and refused to let go.

4

When I woke up this morning, your first one in my home, I felt anguished. I had sat up writing until three o'clock in the morning. Only when I opened my eyes five hours later did I understand what I'd done.

I hadn't thought of it as a kind of violence. But that I'd consciously opted out of giving you food, providing bed linen and a clean towel, while at the same time acting hard and introspective, was a way of committing violence against your person.

All night long you'd slept in the same position. Or not so much slept as lain there utterly passed out. I had evidence for this: when I checked on you in the evening you were lying on your side, half curled up and wedged between two sofa cushions, your head resting in the palm of your hand. When at eight in the morning I went in again, you were still lying in the same position.

It was a good sign, I felt. You couldn't be afraid if you slept so deeply, so immersed in yourself. At least I had satisfied your need for rest, security and recovery, which was demonstrably greater than your need for warmth and food.

I drew this conclusion based on my own experiences.

Whenever there were big changes going on or something was causing anxiety, my own nights used to be haunted by the most terrifying nightmares. Between the ages of eight and twelve I was plagued by recurrent night horrors. Soaked in tears, sweat and pee, I'd bounce out of bed, stand there on the floor still asleep and start taking swings at whatever it was that had come to get me. Or, as a consequence of this nocturnal horror, I'd sit awake in the darkness and stare into nothingness, limp with exhaustion and petrified of passing out and hallucinating more death and isolation.

Your first night in the flat had passed off peacefully. This soothed my nerves. I could have resisted your moving in, I could have said you should stay where you were and we should go on meeting in the daytime as before. I hadn't done that. Which was honourable of me. For this reason, it wasn't right to be too judgemental and harsh on myself now, I reasoned. Of course, I had been a jerk. It was reasonable to feel guilt and remorse about it. But the situation here was new and pressured.

I went into the kitchen, microwaved a coffee, and sat by the window. Hoar frost had formed on the pane of glass. A chill penetrated through the rotten ventilation drum. The mist hung heavy in the shoot-up park, adjacent on the left. Rooftops and pavements were covered in snow.

I should surprise you, it struck me. As soon as you woke up, I'd be ready. I'd tell you we were having a luxury breakfast, and then I'd suggest the buffet at the Hilton. It would catch you off guard. Make you forget the bad things and remember the good.

Which is precisely what happened. When you woke up, I was sitting on the sofa next to you, reading. 'We have to celebrate!' I burst out, pinching your cheek. You sat up on your elbow and gave me a dozy smile. 'What do you say, breakfast at the Hilton? That would be nice, huh? But we have to hurry up. They stop serving in forty.'

Fifteen minutes later we walked into the packed restaurant. Heads turned as the middle classes stared at two tracksuit-wearing dudes: a grown man with a shaved head and a ravaged look about him, and then a boy so eager to get the food down, so greedy as he stormed the buffet with a plate in each hand, that he was roaring with happiness.

5

Two weeks ago, a young man was shot in a street you can see from your window. The man got out of a car and was hit by two bullets, one in his stomach and one in his groin. Social media is awash with a shaky video filmed with a mobile phone from a balcony. Two police officers are squatting over a man lying on the ground, writhing like a worm on a hook. The video is unbearable. The police try to hold him down, to calm him, save his life. Whether you witnessed the attempted murder, whether you stood in your window and saw all this happening, I can't say. I haven't asked you, and you haven't said anything.

You preferred not to leave Nydala. A couple of times per week you would go to the sports centre to play ball, and once a year you went to the Malmö Festival.

Beyond the outer limits of Nydala, the streets, buildings and people you're familiar with, it's as if you're stepping into a force field. You can't see it but you feel it pressing against your body, filling you with unease. To an outsider it seems odd. *Why not leave if the circumstances are limiting you?* For marginalized people the psychology works in the

18

opposite way: *If things are not safe here, in this place where I belong, what would await me on the outside?* In addition to being subjected to violence and humiliation, you'd be confronted with all the things you did not have: money, status, power, social mobility, happiness, freedom.

After that night at the Malmö Festival, I started biking over to your home, meeting you outside the door, giving you lifts to your basketball training sessions to make sure that you got there.

You sat like a little tourist on the back of my bicycle, with your arms around my waist and your head rotating from side to side, captivated by the streets in Malmö that were simultaneously new and well-known, near and out of reach.

It was no coincidence that I took you to the Hilton, the skyscraper downtown, a symbol of luxury and excess. I realize this now. I wanted to break a pattern and set the tone. Now you're with me. Now the streets and their palaces are yours.

Class divisions also cut through the city, the housing projects, where I grew up. The mental barriers could not be shifted. As if there were *No Trespassing* signs lining the roads where the affluent people lived. The milieu was entirely different. Their bodies moving around, fluidly and breezily. Their clothes. Flower beds. Cars. I didn't belong here. And I was terrified that someone would realize, and I'd be kicked out and shown up.

Today I am someone else. I have a full-time job and own my apartment. To some degree I have lost the ability to read the threats and signals, which you're so attuned to.

But I know what I'm seeing when I look at you. When in a room of white people, among dressed-up, well-spoken adults, you crawl back into your shell, seek me out, grow anxious and edgy.

If you are with your friends, you stake out your presence by occupying the space, being loud, disruptive and destructive. You behave like a bunch of arseholes when you move in a flock, or when you take over a public space. Or when you feel that someone is looking down at you.

I used to be tough as well when I was in that flock. Broke things, made adults flare up, behaved like a pig, stole, yelled and fitted into the image of me that had been formed in the world outside. Now, instead, I am the adult who's watching, observing an insecure, frightened bunch of young men who give off an impression of being dangerous – and who *are* dangerous, if pushed. It turns me cold. I don't know how to behave. They're the same as me, I know what they're doing. Maybe for this exact reason I want to put them right, protect them, ask them to shut up.

It's as if they're embarrassing me personally, making me look bad. They make the job of humanizing *blattes* even harder. And it saddens me that they've taken on board what society thinks of them to such a degree that they have to behave in that way. Excluding themselves from all the things that, deep in their hearts, they'd like to be a part of.

6

You started hanging out in the sports hall when you knew I'd be there. And you brought two friends with you, Abbe and Josef.

When I was running training sessions you sometimes stood on the sideline listening attentively, taking in the instructions I was giving, picking up the details and imitating my movements.

You looked so serious about it, performed the moves at such high speed and with so much engagement that people laughed at you.

But you were also the disruptive kids in the sports hall. Loud and horsing around. You were triggered by the smallest of things: one bad pass, one reprimand from a coach, or an unfair decision, and you were capable of flipping. Lashing out and swearing at other kids, but also at grown-ups.

Abbe, who had just been put in foster care, was the instigator. Excess energy crackled around him, and a constant smile bifurcated his face, decorated with a set of braces. With his duality, at the same time devilish and joyously mischievous, he elicited peals of laughter one minute and raging lectures from grown-ups the next.

Abbe's cousin brought him along to the hall for the first time. He was my age, and there was something gloomy in his eyes as he stared tensely down at his mobile phone or turgidly gazed over the children on the court. He wore a bulletproof vest. The strips and straps, which came up over his wishbone, could be seen through his long-arm T-shirt. Once he asked me if there were any jobs going spare, could I hook him up? 'I'm good with kids, like,' he assured me, not very convincingly. Sometime later he was shot in the face not far from my flat in Möllan, but he survived.

Josef was the youngest and quietest of you. He was intelligent, but he bore a darkness inside. He was polite without being ingratiating. And possibly the most stunning basketball talent I've ever seen. Josef's father often picked him up after our training sessions. But I never spoke to him, he always waited in the car by the side of the road.

All three of you have great talent. Abbe is lightning quick, although quite short. You're a bit podgy, but on the other hand you're quick as a weasel and your skill with the ball is like none other in your age group. But Josef trumps you both. He's expected to grow slightly over two metres tall. He has long limbs – he consists more of extremities than body – and he can already dunk high baskets even though he hasn't even turned thirteen. Your range of attributes – mainly down to the fact that you are *blattes* in a white, middle-class environment – make you the black sheep of your respective teams. You stand out because you behave badly; you behave badly because you stand out.

To defuse and prevent conflict I usually gathered the three

of you by the side basket at the far end of the hall, and then challenged you to matches, one on one. We could play for hours. With high, almost violent, intensity. You snorted with fury when you failed to beat a grown man. But because we went on playing together, I gradually gained your confidence.

Often after the three of you had been thrown out of the hall we sat for a long while talking in the changing rooms. You opened up about all sorts of things in life. Afterwards I took you into town. We had kebabs in Möllan Square and we laughed about the hysterical yells of the market vendors, we hung out in the parks, and we played pick-up on outside courts around Malmö. I had you in my grip.

7

I've known for a long time that things were difficult for you at home. I've run into her in the sports hall, but I've kept out of the way, avoided contact.

Your mother has engaged herself a lot in your sports. I'm also aware of that. She talks to the coaches, makes sure that you can go to the training camps, but she also causes problems.

During the games she sometimes starts clapping at the wrong moment, cheers abruptly with no connection to what's happening on the court. Once she fell asleep during one of your games. You ran desperately along the sideline, calling out: 'Wake up, Mum! Wake up!' Your teammates' parents frown at her, the children titter and whisper about her. When I see things like this, I get furious, I break out in a cold sweat. I despise the grown-ups who judge both you and her. And I despise myself for staying passive, for not doing anything about it.

You lack the language and knowledge to make sense of your world. I can see how it torments you, but I don't jump to help you with it. When you're filled with this anxiety of not having the words, I pull back. I grow watchful and closed off. I focus on what we have made up our minds to do: train, train, train.

Until this winter, that is, when everything changed.

You grew morose and remote. Not during the training or when I gave you my attention. At those times you were normal. But as soon as your thoughts weren't kept busy, they quickly drifted off in search of your mother. There was an anxiety about her health, and it felt to me that you'd normalized her issues and become co-dependent. And that your only way out was to make a break with her.

It was a good sign. A necessary liberation. But also an ill omen, as you would need to compensate for the loss and seek out a substitute.

I'd seen it before. Children from dysfunctional families test the water sooner or later; assess whether they dare let go of their lifebuoy once they've caught sight of another. They fix their gaze on you and start swimming.

I was constantly on my toes. If there were the slightest indication that you needed more of me, I'd take action. Resolutely, both with words and actions, I would make it clear: this far but no further. It simply had to be done. I had to stay on my toes, sensitive, adapting my distance to you according to your growing desperation. If you grew too clingy, I'd cut all contact, keep my head down for a few weeks or a month, blow off on answering your messages or showing up in places where we risked running into each other. In this way I'd give rise to a certain insecurity in you, establishing a crack between us, awakening the feeling of alienation. If, in your awkward way, you looked for intimate conversations,

I'd change the subject, make a joke of it, and leave. This would hurt your feelings, but you'd get the idea and accept the reality. No human being has ever been a constant in your life, you have no one to lean on. You don't trust anyone. Not even yourself. And for this reason, I persuaded myself, you'd quickly get over my betrayal.

Nothing went as planned. When it came to it, I was the one who opened up.

It was a Friday night. The usual banter at the sports hall. We were sitting on the long bench by the handball goal, after a session, getting changed. You were quiet and introspective. You'd pulled the hoodie over your head, and you sat leaning forward, tying your shoelaces.

I had an impulse. 'What's up, bro?' I asked.

'It's all good, bro,' you answered quickly, and went on tying your laces.

I put my hand on your shoulder. 'How are you doing for real, Elijah?' I said.

You stopped. Slowly you straightened up and looked into my eyes. Then you burst into tears. Your face contorted and tears ran down your cheeks. I'd never seen you cry before. Your chest convulsed as you tried to catch your breath. Your lower lip trembled. I hugged you, and you cried on my shoulder. After we let go of one another you went on crying, without shielding your face.

At the same time, the women's team was training in the sports hall. Two of the girls by the nearest basket stopped. They stared at you. Not only was there a person crying right next to them, but this person – a thirteen-year-old teenage boy – was making no effort to hide their sorrow. I noticed them. I saw how in your most vulnerable state, you were being watched by strangers. It made something rupture inside of me as well.

'Actually, it's not going so good, Nick,' you sobbed. 'Not so good at all. It's Mum. And it makes me so damn sad, Nick. I want her to feel good, but it's like whatever's going on with her is more important than everything else, more important than me.'

'I understand,' I said. 'I understand it's hard. And it's brave of you to tell me about it. It's good that you tell her how you're doing, how it makes you feel.'

'Yeah,' you said. 'But it doesn't help. She just says, "Yeah, yeah, I know, but it's not so bad." Or she says she's going to get better soon, but she has so much going on at work. Sometimes I don't want to go home. Sometimes I just want to stay out at night and only come home once she's fallen asleep, or not even come home at all. I can't handle it any more.'

'I get it, it's hard,' I said. We fell into silence.

Then I said: 'Maybe I should talk to her. Would you like me to? We can talk to her together. Maybe then she'd realize that I'm here, that I'm backing you up, backing you both up. And that she can come to me if anything comes up. We could tell her you can spend more time with me, to give her some space. What would you say about that?'

You looked at me, took a deep breath. 'Can I?' you said.

'Yeah,' I said. 'Course you can.'

27

'Maybe I can hang with you on weekends,' you said. 'When there's no school and stuff.'

'Yeah,' I said. 'We can sort that out.'

'Maybe I can stay over with you after we've had a game, and then clear off in the morning.'

'Yeah,' I said, 'we have to talk about all this with your mum.'

You wiped your tears away with the sleeve of your jacket. 'Do you feel better now?'

'Yeah,' you said. 'It feels better.'

8

The lift wasn't working, so we walked up the six flights of stairs to your apartment. You were giggly. Cycling out from town in the pouring, cold rain, you'd talked incessantly. I thought that you were nervous of my meeting with your mother affecting my perception of you. My thoughts were elsewhere. It had begun to clarify for me what my visit was really about, and on what basis it was taking place. I was not only there to talk to her, win her trust and offer my support. I realized that I was there to push her into a corner where she was most vulnerable, in her own home, and confront her with the reality that she was letting down her child. One could also see it this way. As the beginnings of an abduction, a planned snatch, with myself as the kidnapper of her son.

If she caused a fuss about it, she'd risk pushing you away even more.

Your mother didn't stand a chance. I'd told you that my home was at your disposal for one weekend day per week. But I knew it was only a matter of time before you started staying over also on weekdays.

* * *

'We're home!' you called out as you opened the front door. Quickly you took off your jacket, stepped out of your shoes and padded into the kitchen. I stood there on the doormat, looking around. The flat was dimly lit and neatly arranged. On the walls were pictures and photos of you, on the sideboard and small table there were ornaments. It was homely and freshly cleaned, smelled of detergent and cigarette smoke. She appeared in the doorway to the kitchen.

'Hi,' she said. 'So you must be Nick? Elijah's talked so much about you.' Her hair hung free, her face was discreetly made up and she wore a light blue blouse and blue denims. She was beautiful, in an older woman sort of way.

'Hi,' I said. 'Yeah, that's right. Nice to meet you.' I stepped forward and shook her hand.

'Would you like anything to eat or drink?' she asked.

'No thanks,' I said. You stood by the sink, and you'd just swept down a glass of water. Your eyes went back and forth between your mother and me. I pulled out a chair and took a seat while you took two slices of bread from a bag and put them in the toaster. Your mother stood by the open balcony door and lit a cigarette.

We did some small talk, the nasty weather, Nydala, what it was like living here, your school, your friends. 'They're nice boys,' she said. 'I like them all. Especially Radi. But they probably get up to a lot of no good as well.' She tittered.

'No good,' you said. 'No one says no good, Mum. Plus, Radi doesn't get into anything, he's real smart.'

'Yeah, I know,' she said. 'He's a good lad. I'm just a bit hung up about how there's so little to do around here.'

There was a silence. Two pieces of toast shot up with a rattling sound. You put them on the draining board, spread butter over them and smeared on a spoon of marmalade.

'Mum,' you said. 'Me and Nick have something we want to talk to you about. That thing I told you before, our idea.'

'Oh yeah, that's right,' she said with a laugh. She pulled the balcony door shut and stubbed out her cigarette in an ashtray on the windowsill. The stifling smell of smoke welled over me.

She crossed her arms. 'You're worried about me,' she said. 'But you don't have to worry, I've told you. It's not as if I haven't got the situation under control.'

'You don't have control of anything, Mum,' you said, raising your voice. 'Don't lie! I'm really worried.'

'But you don't have to be worried, darling,' she said, 'it's not as bad as you say.'

'You're lying,' you said. 'And if things don't change, I don't want to live here any more.'

You looked at me. None of that mischief of yours was left in your eyes. Only anxiety and desperation.

Your mother turned around and took a step towards the window. I stood up and went to the draining board, took a glass from the drying rack and filled it with water.

'Nick . . .' you said, then stopped yourself.

I took over. 'Maybe it's best if your mum and I have a word, just the two of us,' I said. 'Is that okay for you?' You nodded. Took your toast and left the room with your head down.

Outside the window it was pitch black. The wind whined. Rain ran in streaks down the glass, smattering against the windowsill. Your mother's face had changed. This was no longer a pleasant visit.

'I understand that this is hard,' I said. 'But I'm here to try to support you, both you and Elijah. I've known him for so many years and he trusts me.'

She spun around. Pulled out a chair and sank down heavily on it. 'He's . . . just so sensitive,' she said, without looking at me. 'Sure, maybe I have problems, but who doesn't? I have some things I need to solve right now.'

'But that's what we wanted to say,' I said. 'If Elijah spends more time with me in the city, and gets away from the area around here, you get more time to focus on yourself. It's not as if he'll be away for ever. I've told him he can do a sleepover at my place on the weekends if he wants to. Then he'll be here the rest of the time. If that's okay with you, I mean.'

'Yeah,' she said. 'He does what he wants. I just don't understand why he's getting so worked up about it. I do everything for him, I always have done, and he knows it.' She started crying and I was unsure whether I should comfort her.

'I know,' I tried. 'I know how much you do for him. How much you have been involved in his life, his basketball. And he loves you and wants you to be happy.'

'Yeah,' she said, tearing a piece of kitchen roll and blowing her nose. 'Who doesn't.' She stood up and opened the balcony door. Tapped a cigarette out of the pack, lit it, and blew the smoke out of the crack. She looked at me. 'I love him more than life itself. You know that? He's my everything.

It's always been just the two of us. That's how it's been. But if he wants to stay with you, he may. He's old enough to make his own decisions. I'll be all right.'

9

One afternoon when I was ten years old, I saw my mother standing in the hall with a girl I didn't know. My memory of it is crystal clear. Mum has just taken our dog Muffin off the lead and he darts past my room as I stick my head out of the doorway. Mum has her usual aura of freshness around her, which she gets when she has been outside for a long time. Her streaked grey hair is plastered over her face, dampened by the rain. And at her side, gazing down at the floor, stands a girl. Drops of water from their raincoats are collecting on the doormat by their feet. Mum is wearing heavy-duty military green Wellingtons, the girl has a pair of drenched trainers on. The girl exudes nature and open skies. She has jet-black hair, a vague hint of a moustache on her upper lip, and her eyes are narrow and black.

'Who's she?' I ask, pointing at the girl.

'This is my friend,' says Mum. 'Her name is Anja. I have told you about Anja, haven't I?' Mum puts her arm round the girl's shoulder. 'Anja often comes with me on my walkies. Muffin adores her.'

'What's she doing here?' I manage to blurt out, reeling with jealousy.

'She's here because she's my friend, I already told you. And because she's having dinner with us tonight.'

Anja is Russian, I find out soon enough. But not Russian like the Russians I know about or have seen on television. She's more Asiatic than pale-skinned European. And unlike those of my friends whose parents are Iranian, Kurdish, Thai, Nigerian or Turkish, Anja is a *blatte* for real – maladjusted, sort of knocked about, with an odd style of dressing as if she just got off the boat.

It doesn't take long before Anja's singularities come to light. The social norms and codes of behaviour in our area are set in stone. From an early age I have learned to read and incorporate them into my personality, identity, body language and my expectations of others. Everything I do, the person I am, corresponds to a pattern and acquired logic. Girls are like this, guys are like that. Whether one is a Swedie or a *blatte* is also a part of the equation, as well as one's age, and the places one frequents or avoids at various times of the day. Corpulence, having a harelip, being cross-eyed, ears sticking out, acne, a bum-fluff moustache, family connections, one's home address – everything is evaluated and categorized and can be used against you. Threatening the order of things is a displacement of everyone's existence. It leads to repercussions.

As far as Anja is concerned, the rules are irrelevant, in suspension. Constantly she crosses the boundaries. She socializes freely with adults. She likes wrestling. She's heavy-handed to the point of violence. She talks in a shrill voice and laughs with a shriek, like a mule. Overwhelmed by sudden emotions, she kisses me and my brother. When we move away with a pretence of disgust, she winks at Mum. Anja is wild, beautiful and free. I envy her lack of constraint and I want to be like her.

When my mother is there, Anja is untouchable. She makes that clear to us from the very beginning, wagging her finger at us: 'Anja is with me. Do you hear? Don't you mess with her.' This favouritism hurts my feelings. But I understand that my mother is crossing boundaries too, taking risks. Her efforts on behalf of Anja, a stranger's child, contravene the unwritten rules. It's heterodox and dubious and may lead to gossip. Mum is helping a child in need. Obviously, I also know this. She's doing the right thing and I feel proud of her.

Soon, Anja's situation is clarified. Her parents have newly separated. The father has found another woman and left his family.

When I come home from school one day, Anja's mother is sitting in our kitchen in floods of tears. She smokes my mum's cigarettes and chews on long chalk crayons, which form a white mush in her mouth. The more chalk she eats, the more her voice turns hoarse. She howls without self-restraint. Makes long telephone calls to her home country, which costs my mother thousands of kronor in telephone bills. Mum wanders between the rooms. So stressed is she about these unforeseen, ticking charges, and this chalk-munching howling woman who has annexed her kitchen, that she starts talking to herself.

Anja is apparently unaffected by her mother's crazy antics. As I walk into my room I find her sitting there, playing with my action figures. She titters; she's drawn big cocks on my desk in pencil. I don't like her being here. It's not about her. I'm fine with Anja. She's like a sister to me. But there's talk in the area that my mum is socializing with other people's kids. And apparently Pippi Longstocking has moved in.

10

That first week after our visit to your mother you stayed the night here between Saturday and Sunday. The following two weeks you stayed Friday to Sunday. This week: all week.

Routines have been established. I've given you the spare keys to the apartment. You dump your bag after school, pack your training clothes and head off. In the evenings we meet in the city in time for dinner. I never cook. Either we go into one of the small restaurants close to the apartment or we get a takeaway.

One might think eating out would be excessively expensive. But in Möllan one is spoiled for choice with restaurants, and the prices are kept very low by having badly paid staff, often illegal immigrants. One can get a decent bit of chow here for around sixty kronor a plate. Our dinner conversations are long; we talk about the day that's gone by. I ask questions and you babble away. If it's a weekend, we see each other all day, training or sitting in cafes until it gets dark outside. Before midnight, with the precision of a chronograph, you lie utterly knocked out on the sofa. On weekday afternoons and evenings, when we're both at home, I keep to the bedroom or the kitchen, whereas you sit at the computer in the living room. You're restless and pining for company but you have understood the basic set-up, and you leave me in peace.

Since you moved in we have hardly mentioned your mother. I feel sympathy for her.

I don't know what is going to happen with my finances. I worry how long this will go on. Are you going to ruin me? Maybe it's a little much to ask, expecting money from someone whose child one has kidnapped. But I encourage you to keep trying. When you ask me for small change for the bus or a hundred kronor to top up the phone, I give you the money reluctantly, then arrange a sour face and tell you that you have to talk to your mother. It's costing me at least three thousand kronor per month paying for your keep, that's what I've worked out. This is not an insignificant sum, not for me. It means I have to cut down on shopping for clothes; overseas travel is out of the question. Yet by giving you a bad conscience, I can: A. project my irritation. B. hold on to my position of power. C. get you to tell your mother about the sacrifices I am making, making her feel guilty so that she forgets I have abducted her son.

11

It was my birthday yesterday. I didn't tell you, so that you wouldn't feel compelled to buy me a present or lay on some festivities. But it didn't take you many hours from waking up to foil my plans. Facebook gave me away. I heard you cry out from the living room: 'Nick, it says here it's your birthday today!' Then you hopped off your chair with a thump and ran to me in the kitchen. You were puzzled – as if this news that had reached your ears simply couldn't be true.

'Yeah,' I said, 'that's right. But it's no big deal, I don't want us to make a big deal of it, okay?'

'Not make a big deal of it?' you said, almost yelling. 'But it is a big deal, Nick! It's your birthday!' You left the kitchen, put on your gear in the hall and popped your head through the doorway. 'I'm heading out. I'll be back soon.'

'Aren't you going to wish me a happy birthday first?' I said.

'That's right,' you said with a grin. 'Happy birthday, Nick. It's mad sweet it's your birthday.'

Seconds later I saw you running across the street. Legging it as if someone were chasing you, cutting across the lawns of the shoot-up park, then heading right towards Triangeln's mall.

I sat there for a long time with my cup of coffee in my hand. *This is not good*, I thought to myself. *This is not fucking good.* When your eyes glitter like that you're capable of anything. That determination, something maniacal in your gaze, is ominous. Your eyes don't express exultation or joy. There's something sharp in them, something out of reach and almost merciless. You have a goal in sight. And if the sky has to be torn down to reach your goal, then the sky will be torn down.

How many times have I met that gaze and thought to myself that things are about to fall apart?

How many times has that gaze not been the precursor to absolute disaster?

Last summer, when you took part in the basketball training camp, North West Camp in Ängelholm, was one such occasion. I had paid the participant's fee of almost two thousand kronor. It was going to be your first real basketball trip, and in the car on the way up your excitement was already very high. But once we got there and stood in the exuberant line of parents and kids with their big bags and just-purchased basketballs under their arms, your mood was something altogether different. You were serious and taciturn. You looked around, then looked at me, your eyes as black as glass.

Damn it, I thought to myself as I hugged you. On the way back to the car, I called the person in charge of the camp. I presented myself, told them that a boy called Elijah had just checked in, and it would be good if they established a connection to him at an early stage, as he had special needs.

'How do you mean?' the man said.

'Well,' I said, 'he's a bit of an attention-seeker, which you'll notice. So, if his visit is going to work out, you'll probably have to back him up a little more and establish some boundaries.'

The man said, 'Is he on the spectrum?'

'No,' I said. 'He's totally normal. But he's thirteen, explosive, and can sometimes be a bit domineering.'

'What was his name again?' said the man.

'Elijah,' I said. 'Elijah Clarance. He's a good kid. Plus, a huge talent. It's just that he can be a bit over the top.'

'Yeah, sure,' the man said. 'But we can't give special treatment to any of the participants. We have rules and they have to be respected by everyone.'

'I understand that,' I said. 'I just thought you needed to know.'

'Yeah,' he said. 'It's good that you informed us. I'll get in touch if anything comes up.'

Which he did. Old bastard.

He called about an hour later, more dejected than irritated. He sighed. 'You'll have to come pick him up. It's not going to work. You can't keep that kid in furnished rooms.'

Now I was worried about what would happen next, how you would choose to highlight the occasion. You had no money.

Once you came back, we went to the square in Möllan to celebrate. Abbe and Josef came with us. As we crossed the square, you got it into your heads to sing for me. You screeched like a bunch of drunkards, and the more noise you made with your pubescent crowing, the more you laughed. Shit, I felt so embarrassed.

We ordered double portions at Chicken Cottage. Your faces glistened with chicken fat. I found myself constantly glancing at the badly wrapped present, which was sticking out of your jacket pocket. It consisted more of adhesive tape than wrapping paper. *The cops will be after us*, I thought. *You've stolen something and ended up on some surveillance camera. It's all over.*

'Are you going to let me open my present or what?' I said halfway through our meal.

'Sure thing, Nick,' you said, hauling out the package. 'Happy birthday!'

You handed it over and I tore off the paper. Once I saw what it was, I burst out laughing. Socks. A ten-pack of black ankle-length socks from Intersport. The budget variety. A hundred kronor per package.

I laughed so hard that I got tears in my eyes. You twisted uneasily. Abbe smiled, put his hand on your shoulder, became the grown-up in the room. 'It's a really good present, bro,' he said. 'You can't ever have too many socks.'

'Yes,' I said, choking even more. 'This is sweet, bro, thanks so much.'

'But it was good, right, Nick?' you said. 'You said you needed new socks?'

'Yeah, bro,' I said. 'It's perfect. It's just what I wanted.'

12

'Nick, I got a pretty good mark on my book review!'

'What book review?'

'That one about *The Evil.*'

'Aha, cool. You got it?'

'Yeah, it's in my bag.'

'Is it okay if I have a look at it?'

'Course. One thing the teacher said was I gave a bit too much away. In a review you're supposed to draw people in, not give away the most important thing.'

'No, she's right about that.'

'Yeah. Check this. She liked this bit especially.'

At the beginning the weather is a bit grey but then it brightens up, more happy-like and positive. But it feels like when all the negative things happen the weather changes again to a grey, dark, slightly negative atmosphere.

'You see? She has written "Yes!" there.'

'I can see why. It's really good.'

'Then she wrote her comments here.'

Develop the opinion section after condensing the action part. Do not forget to comment on what you thought about the actors-performances !

'The actors' performances?'

'Yeah?'

'What does she mean by that?'

'What do you mean, what does she mean?'

'Did you read the book or did you watch the movie?'

'Oh, no, no, we never read it. We'd never have time for that, she said. So we ended up watching the movie.'

'Aha, but it says "Book-review"?'

'Yeah, exactly, that was the assignment. It was really good, like. Have you seen it?'

'No. I haven't. It's probably good. The book is good.'

'Yeah, I'm sure. I mean, the film was really good. For a Swedish film.'

'I can imagine. But . . . that teacher, is she really your Swedish teacher?'

'Yeah, yeah, she's our Swedish teacher. She's cool. Why?'

'Is she Swedish? Like, a Swedie?'

'Yeah, yeah, course she's a Swedie.'

'Okay, because the way she writes is a bit messed up.'

'Messed up? How do you mean?'

'Well, that last sentence is not entirely correct, for instance.'

'How do you mean?'

'I see three errors in that sentence. Can you see them?'

'No? Or I mean . . . no. Where?'

'Let's start with your heading. You've written Book-review. You see? But it's not hyphenated, it's written as two words: Book Review. The way it's pronounced.'

'Uh-huh. Yeah. That's true.'

'And she hasn't pointed that out. Then she makes a similar

error herself a little further down, when she writes "actors-performances". You see it?'

'Yeah, I see that. She's put a dash in the middle but it should be two words. Like the way it's spoken. You're supposed to say it separately. Actors *pause* performances, not actors-performances.'

'Yeah, that's exactly right. Then there are two other mistakes. You see them?'

'No . . .'

'How do you write the actors bit? Isn't it supposed to have an apostrophe? The actors' performances, like, the performances of the actors?'

'Oh yeah, of course.'

'Yeah. Can you see the last mistake?'

'No.'

'The exclamation mark?'

'No . . . Or, I mean, yeah . . . yes! I can see it. There shouldn't be a space there, the exclamation mark should come right after the "s". Like it's a part of the word. Right?'

'Exactly.'

'Yeah. Ha-ha. I mean, shit. I'll tell her. I'll smoke her out tomorrow. Ha-ha. Can I smoke her out, Nick?'

13

First of May.

We counted the vomit stains on the way to the Greek joint: four. We ordered lunch. And just as the chicken kebabs with brown-roasted potato wedges and a dollop of fatty tzatziki were placed on the table, the red-dressed procession passed by outside, on the other side of the fogged-up windows.

The Swedies, I thought to myself, drum and chant and pump their fists for justice. While the *blattes* stand about on the pavement or watch the demonstrators from their apartments. Staring at the circus passing by, like fish in their aquariums. With equal portions of envy, ridicule and disdain. I was never able to take part in those demonstrations. Every time, I felt out of place, I stopped myself from joining in.

Then I got to thinking about an event that happened almost two decades ago, an event that I seemed to have repressed or hadn't had the occasion to remember, until that exact day in the Greek restaurant on this May Day.

The memory was triggered by a question you'd asked over dinner the night before. Out of nowhere you wondered how old I was the first time I had sex. I was offended. To the extent that I almost felt like smashing your plate on the floor and chewing you out.

Now, thinking back on it, I can't quite remember why I reacted so strongly. I know what occupies your mind, what you as a boy in your first teenage years are going through. The metamorphosis. This wholly new version of you which is emerging and delineated in your more and more defined muscles, standing there flexing yourself in front of the mirror in the evenings, with a bare torso and a flaming red face. You're on your way to becoming a man. You are popular among some of the children around you and feared by others. You're discovering that you can make use of these advantages, of which previously you had no notion. Exactly how you do this is still unclear, and that is why you turn to me.

The conversations are difficult because I find it repugnant to think of you as a sexual creature. And it is quite clear that the little monster which, in real time, is pushing out from beneath the layers of boyish fat is engaged in the full enactment of its being. It's easily done, fantasizing about how you, through the various stages between boy and man, and thereafter, will plough through the field of human objects before you.

You have still not gone into action. Your animality is enclosed within you like the rumbling precursors to a volcanic eruption in a mountain. But in due course it will erupt. Nothing that I do or say can prevent it.

Like you, I came late to puberty. My friends had body hair, downy soft moustaches, male voices long before me. One by one they grew indecipherably ruttish, full of surplus energy, with hairy cocks that stood up in the showers after gym practice. I became insecure about myself, my body, and my pathetic, unserviceable, hairless genitalia. Until even I was transformed and nothing was ever quite the same.

I never knew in the mornings who I was about to meet in the mirror. Suddenly my face was deformed by flaring spots and greasy skin, my hair was oily and spattered with white dandruff, bum-fluff covered my upper lip, and my voice deepened by a few octaves. As for my cock, which until then I'd mostly noticed and fiddled with out of curiosity and to pass the time – what manner of strange, dangling appendage was this? – now became the object around which everything revolved, surrounded by shame and pleasure.

As a consequence of my late physical development, I grew obsessed with other boys' cocks. I was quite capable of standing in my corner of the shower after PE or practice, surreptitiously glancing at them, taking mental notes and studying them with minute attention to detail. It became a compulsive behaviour. Being obsessed as I was in this way about male genitalia soon caused me to draw the logical and alarming conclusion that I had to be gay. Yes, I just had to be gay. Nothing could be more obvious. And once that thought had taken root it was impossible to chase it away.

I went to my mother in a state of anguish. She was always understanding and supportive, but would telling her I thought I might be gay possibly be too much? I mentioned it in passing while she was standing at the stove, cooking.

'Mum,' I said, 'I think I'm becoming gay.'

She stiffened. A second, two seconds, went by. Then she went on stirring the pot: 'There's no possible way you can be sure of that, sweetie. I don't want you to think about it any more.'

The thing that was considered most deviant during my growing up, a cause of violence and exclusion, was homosexuality. To be vulnerable, weak and to be considered effeminate was bad enough, but being gay was more or less the same as being an outlaw. I remember a boy in my area who was rubber-stamped as gay, and his walk to and from school and through its corridors was more or less like the road to Golgotha. We felt sorry for him; we were nice to him when no one was watching. But there was also the fact that any association with him, or for that matter not hitting, spitting at or ridiculing him when the others did, might lead to punishment for acting as an ally.

Contempt for weakness has formed you more than it formed me. Some territorial gains have been made by those of non-normative sexuality. But on the whole, society has grown harsher. Especially for those who break against the norms as you do: because you are Black and a Muslim.

In fact, it's quite possible that you are homosexual or non-binary. I've hardly given any thought to that. In which case it is also quite possible that in some unguarded moment I've said or done something that has made you reject who you are and feel even more self-loathing. Or that you've just picked up some signalling from my way of being, and how I wish to present myself as a man. That my swagger has put me out of reach for conversations about what you may have begun to despise in yourself. Is that how it is?

* * *

You're in the first, chaotic teenage years. You turn to me because you need to vent your feelings. You confide in me what is most private and shameful. It's a fine thing. But as we sat there at the dining table, our gobs full of chicken, I did not want to talk about sex, even less so about my own sex life. I had the sense not to reflect any shame onto you or to get annoyed, so I merely answered evasively: 'At your age I'd had dealings with a girl for quite a long time, and, once we felt ready to go the whole way, we did it. We were careful about using contraceptives and we discussed our decision.' You stared at me. Your eyes were blank with disinterest. I avoided any filth and made myself sound like a sex education teacher. And so the conversation died.

But the emotions had been stirred. And an event that took place two decades earlier swept into my conscious mind.

This is what I remembered.

14

We're lying on the roof of the bicycle shed, my friend Hamid and I, cooling ourselves in the shade of a tree. It's summer. The afternoon sun cuts streaks of light through the foliage. The day, which has been full of activity, is almost at an end. Stillness has descended.

Then, suddenly, the spell is broken by a shrill voice from the ground beneath us. It's the boy next door, Adam. We creep up to the edge and look down. Adam is leaning forward, red-faced, and trying to catch his breath. He points towards the near-lying courtyard and hisses, 'They're fucking over there! They're fucking! They're fucking!'

Quickly we get to our feet and slide down into the flower bed. And before Adam has even had time to collect himself and come along, we're out of sight. We run towards the tall bushes and lush trees that separate the courtyards. Thread our way through the well-trodden passage, scratch ourselves on thorns, and emerge on the other side with arms flailing. At the other end of the courtyard, climbed onto the roof of the refuse building, or sitting on top of the peeling green fence, we see a gang of about ten or twelve kids. They're laughing and yelling, excitedly shoving each other, their eyes fixed on the grass. We pick up speed. Run across the yellow lawn and reach the refuse hut and then, with practised movements, climb the drainpipe and heave ourselves over the edge. Trembling after the rush, with the flimsy corrugated roof buckling under my feet, I totter forward. I settle in between the bodies and when I lean forward, I feel my head reeling. Two children are lying naked down there. A boy and a girl. I can see the boy's speckled back, his buttocks, the back of his long, slender legs. And beneath him, the outstretched limbs of the girl.

My neighbour, Baha, standing right beside me, has taken charge of the situation with screeching and wild gestures. Threatening to beat them if they stop, and promising to reward them in the form of sweets if they obey his command to continue, he gets out a bag and flings down handfuls of them, and in this way forces them to assault one another. A sense of anger comes over me. I look at Baha, furious with envy. He does not have the status to put himself at the centre of events, to be the instigator. Baha is a little piece of shit. I want to fly at him. But with a fight one might risk ruining the situation, so I quell the impulse.

The boy in the grass grinds himself against the girl and thrusts his lower body against hers. Baha yells out, 'Fuck her! Fuck her!' He tosses sweets into the grass. Toffees, chewing gum, lollipops, bags of nut crème. The boy thrusts harder and harder. Thrusts and scrabbles together his reward into a gravelly little pile. Then his face turns up and I can see who he is.

The boy's name is Martin, he lives in House 4. I don't know him personally, but somehow we all know everyone.

We're at the same school, he's twelve years old and I'm a year older. His father's a drunk with a reputation of being dangerous. His mother is only ever seen as a shadow behind the curtain. Martin may possibly be mentally slow in some way. He slurs his words as if his tongue's in a twist; the words run out of his mouth with saliva. He lacks connections, and because no one will stand up for him, there's no problem treating him in any way one likes, without risk of reprisals. I've hurt him on one or two occasions. Once he asked if he could play basketball with us. On that occasion I slapped his face. Once he strayed into our courtyard and then he was captured by my brother. My brother told me to hold on to him, and he disappeared into the flat. I did as I was asked. Stood there silently with Martin in the courtyard, held on to the sleeve of his jacket. He put up no resistance. Just stood there with his arms limp, his eyes empty and filled with sorrow. My brother came back with a 50 cl plastic bottle filled with dark blue gunk. He handed Martin the bottle, told him it was a magic potion and forced him to drink. Martin drank and was nauseated. Drank and was nauseated. When the bottle was empty, he ran off, crying. The gunk, my brother said laughingly, consisted of dishwasher rinse, ketchup, detergent, spices, vinegar and other things he'd had to hand.

Now, Martin is lying in the grass on top of a girl. My feelings are contradictory. I'm disgusted by him. I'm agitated, exhilarated, nervous.

Martin shifts and I see the girl beneath him.

'Fuck, no!' I yell, drawing back. 'You pigs! You disgusting fucking pigs!'

The girl lies immobile. Her hair is long and orange-yellow, spread like a fan in the dry grass. Her eyes are clear blue, staring into ours. The girl is Martin's sister. She is two years younger than her brother. Her name is Elsa.

Baha yells and issues orders. Sweets rain down over the children. Slowly, the sun goes down behind the rentals blocks of the housing project.

Why do I remember this now, two decades later? Maybe it is because the scene, however clearly it has been etched into my eyes, now takes on a different significance. Now I see it as an adult, with a sense of perspective on my own childhood, my own vulnerability, my stirring sexuality. I see it and I look at you, and I stand to one side as I think of young people's relationships to their own and other people's bodies. About herd mentality, and how kids can commit the most unbearable acts of cruelty against one another.

15

Swedish Public Service Television called and asked if I wanted to take part in a debate. They said it was going to address the subject of gang criminality. I said that it would depend on the presentation and content, and who the other panellists were. The man suggested a meeting at the editorial offices in Western Harbour. Once I was there, he assured me that their intention was to approach the subject with care; *dignity* was the word he used. Then he told me that they would play some short video sequences, which I asked to see. The first was of a veiled woman describing how it was lethal living in her area, and she wanted to move away. The next was of a man, saying that the gang ran everything. And the third clip was that video footage from your area, filmed from a balcony, with the two police and the man thrashing in the street. I turned to the producer, looked at his ugly slit-like glasses. 'What are you doing?' I said. 'You can't show that. Have you considered how that man's family and friends will feel, or others who have experienced something like that?'

I declined to take part in the debate.

* * *

56

Last Thursday I was tormented by a bad headache. It started in the afternoon. I was at the stove, making coffee, when I felt a painful pressure across my forehead. There was a flash, as if I'd had an electric shock, and when I pressed my wrists against my head to even out the pressure, the voltage increased even more and engulfed my entire cranium. I was frightened. I stumbled over to the kitchen table and sank down on a chair and, when I leaned forward and buried my face in my hands, my head started thumping. Or rather: something *inside* of my head, just behind the frontal lobe, started thumping with a hard, rhythmic motion against the soft, sensitive surface of the brain. I thought to myself: *Now I'll die of a brain haemorrhage.*

I didn't recognize the pain, couldn't connect it to any earlier experiences. I have struck my head against hard objects and I've had hard objects strike my head. I've had concussions, my face and scalp have been gouged open. Blood has gushed in spurts from my skull, splattering and running in streams into my eyes and mouth. I have hurt myself without breaking the skin, so that blood has seeped beneath the swelling, smooth, pulsating wound, which has been dyed red, blue and then yellow.

Nowadays I never bleed. My life is arranged in such a way that collisions with the world and the people in it can be predicted and avoided, staved off and evaded. It must be two years ago since I saw my own blood flowing. Which disappoints me to a certain extent because I still think it's cool to bleed. I also find it heavy to tell people that I have bled. Scars and bandages and bruises and thick lips and surgical tape are cool to put on display. I imagine people thinking to themselves: *There goes a hard bastard.* Or at least a person who is careless and risk-taking, with a temper that can flare up and lead to physical conflict. A person who is not afraid of confrontation – in other words someone who keeps his back straight and doesn't take shit. Who gets involved if he sees an injustice being done and pays back when required.

The number of stitches that I've had in my head and face must amount to at least fifty. I see myself at various stages of my life, in front of the mirror, admiring my wounds, my bandages, my temporary disfigurement – which is actually not a disfigurement at all but rather a decoration, an orna- mentation of the face. I see the black sutures hooked through the skin with a needle to close up the gash, like a carelessly sewn-up hole in a pair of trousers. Stitches, which are later ripped out, leaving a line in the skin as enduring as the memory of the event, although it can also be rubbed out by time.

What all of these injuries have in common is that I have always intuitively known that the pain caused by them will pass. I have felt its cause and I have known that it's not dangerous. The same applies to the migraine attacks I've had a few times per year. The cause of the ailment is unknown, and I can't say what triggers my attacks. But I've experienced them so many times and I feel such familiarity with forerunning indicators – the white, sensory and blinding flickering across the field of vision of my right eye, a deadening feeling in my arms, and the hour-long wait before the agonies begin – that I approach the whole thing with a certain rationality: I go to the kitchen and get out my medicine box from the cupboard. Then wash down two 500 mg paracetamol tablets and a 400 mg Ibruprofen with a glass of sugared water. I cancel anything I've got planned in the next two days. Then, I draw all the blinds in the flat and open a window. I lie down on the bed with a wet towel over my face and disappear into the mist.

Thursday's headache came entirely without warning. I leaned over the kitchen table, writhing in agony. Then I picked up the telephone and called 112. 'I think I may have had a brain haemorrhage,' I said to the woman at the other end of the line. 'You have to come, I think I've had a brain haemorrhage.' I don't remember what the woman asked me. I remember a remote, tinny voice, and I gave my name and my address. Then I must have put the receiver on the table and fallen asleep or passed out, because in the next second I heard sirens. First from afar, as if in a dream. Then closer, as I was coming to. When the ambulance swung into my street, I opened my eyes and I was absolutely clear. *They're coming here*, I thought. *They've come for me.* The sirens rebounded between the walls of the houses, deafeningly loud. Then deafeningly silent when they abruptly turned them off.

The doors of the ambulance were opened and closed, and the front entrance was pushed wide. I stood up and teetered over to the sink. I filled the empty coffee cup with water and drank a mouthful. My head felt lighter, I realized. It still hurt but it wasn't as terrible as before. Thudding steps in the stairwell, a slight feeling of panic. Fists thumping on the door. I could just fuck off opening it and hope they clear off. It was a futile thought. They wouldn't just leave. They'd been informed that someone had suffered a brain haemorrhage. They were emergency medics, not TV licence people. So I opened the door.

On the other side stood a man and a woman, both of them tall. They looked at me, amazed. 'Hi,' I said. 'I'm okay now. I just had such a splitting headache.'

'There was something about a stroke,' said the man.

'No,' I said. 'Just a brain haemorrhage. That's how it felt. But it feels better now.'

They looked at each other. Looked at me. 'Better take a look at you,' said the man.

'Yeah,' I said, 'come in.'

They asked me to sit on the sofa. The woman fidgeted inside a bag of instruments, then stopped herself. She asked how I was feeling, whether I'd had problems before, how I felt earlier. I told her while the man looked out of the open balcony door.

'It could be the weather,' he said without looking at me. 'Have you thought about that?' He turned to the woman.

'Yes,' she said. 'He's so young. It's probably just the weather. It's been so unsettled, thunder in the air, a charged atmosphere. We had a similar call a week or so back. But it's nothing dangerous.'

'The weather?' I said.

'Yeah,' said the man. 'Biological weather. That's what it's called. Or biometeorology. People don't bring it up very much, but we're very affected by it. Things can get especially unstable when it's very hot.'

I looked at the sky. It was grey or light grey at the top, then black at the lower end. The wind was picking up, tearing at the trees and pressing into the buildings. Clouds rolled in over the rooftops in massive mountainous formations, indicating rain.

After the emergency services team had left and the pouring rain and thunder drew in over the city, I sat on the sofa and pondered on what had happened. I should have been embarrassed. I'd called for an ambulance after mistaking a normal headache for a brain haemorrhage; really I should have been consumed by the most excruciating shame. But I wasn't. I felt calm. At peace.

It's strange. I can barely let someone hold the door open for me or even be helped by a shop assistant without a feeling of awkwardness. Partly because of the invasive intimacy of some stranger offering their service. And partly because of the insecurity that arises: am I inferior or superior?

In contact with service staff the feeling is manageable as their professional status is low, and I am familiar with the customs, language and jargon of the working classes. In case of any conflict, they too can't have any particular expectations of support from society. We are equally matched opponents.

It's worse when one is dealing with people from the higher social classes or professions that command respect. Such as officers of the law. On occasions when I have been stopped and frisked by the police, forced to stand with my legs apart while they slide their hands over my body, my groin and my genitals, panic has welled up within me. Sometimes it's been so strong that I've had to engage all my willpower just to stop myself from putting up a fight or trying to escape. And then afterwards, as I've shuffled off, shaking, humiliated and cut down to size, the feeling of hatred and impotence has made me want to cry.

I wasn't feeling as low as I should have been. I had slumped there over the kitchen table like some hypochondriac, thinking to myself that I was going to die. The thought of it made me smile.

And then I remembered another thought that had run through me in my moment of imaginary death. I wanted you to come home.

As my brain thumped and fear came washing over me, I hoped you'd walk in through the front door and greet me. I imagined how you'd continue into the kitchen. Then stop yourself when you saw me lying there, lifeless, standing in silence for a moment, in icy confusion, and then whisper: 'Nick, are you okay?' And when there was no answer, you'd rush forward and shake me, yelling into my ear: 'Nick! Can you hear me! Wake up, Nick!' After a lot of shaking and yelling, with tears clogging your throat, you'd call the emergency services. 'He's just lying there on the table,' you'd say in a broken voice. 'He doesn't answer, he's just out of it, you have to send an ambulance!'

The monotonous voice of the operator would require you to describe calmly and clearly what had happened. But you wouldn't be calm and clear. And when the voice didn't respond to your urgency, didn't seem to be taking it seriously, you'd cry out: 'Don't you get it? He doesn't answer when I call him, he just lies there. You have to come, please!'

The operator would ask you to take it easy and describe everything. You'd have to repeat what you'd already said. Following that, the operator would ask for a name and address.

But you don't know the address you're living at. So, you wouldn't be able to answer that question. Actually, you don't even know what it says on the letter box. Lunabba – you do know this is my surname. But you can't pronounce it properly or spell it. By now you'd be increasingly desperate, yelling out: 'I don't know, I don't know the address. But please come, we're in the city, in Möllan, just by the Greek diner!'

Or else you'd have come into the kitchen to find me lying across the table in terrible pain, still conscious, but hardly able to speak. It would frighten you because you've never seen me weak or in need. I'd see the terror in your eyes, hear your faint, quivering voice: 'What's up with you Nick, why are you like this? What's happened?' You'd put your hand on my shoulder to console me. 'Everything is going to be okay, Nick, I promise. Everything is going to be okay.'

I'd play along with your fears. 'No, brother. I'm not so sure it's going to be okay. Not this time. I feel as if my brain is expanding, as if I'm going to have a brain haemorrhage. I don't think I'm going to survive it.'

'Don't say that, Nick,' you'd say. 'Please don't say that.'

'You have to promise me one thing, Elijah,' I'd whisper. 'Promise me that you'll live a long and wonderful life.

63

Promise me that. Promise not to be afraid of loving someone. Don't repeat my mistake. Love a lot, don't hold back. You're the best person I've ever met. I'm so glad you came into my life, Elijah. You're my kid, never forget it. Live a wonderful life. I love you . . .'

I'd close my eyes, sinking down with my cheek against the tabletop.

'Nick?' Your voice like a lost surge of breath. 'Nick? Nick! Hey, wake up! Wake up dammit. Please, Nick! Don't leave me. I can't make it without you.'

16

The other day you asked if it wasn't time for us to get you a bed, or at least a mattress.

I couldn't understand what you meant by that. 'What's wrong with where you're sleeping?'

You've been sleeping on the sofa for so long that I've stopped thinking about it, I've got used to the thought.

You, on the other hand, had been pondering on it for a while, I realized. Maybe afraid to bring it up in case you stirred my anger.

You did stir my anger. I felt mean. And, in my usual way, I transferred my feelings of guilt onto you.

'Yeah, yeah,' I said. 'Let's do it once the finances allow it. But as things are now, I hardly have money to put food on the table.'

The living room never goes entirely dark at night. The glare of the street light outside shines through the blinds, and so you sleep in a grey haze.

In addition, the apartment becomes cold in spring, autumn and winter. I haven't managed to locate the problem. The radiators don't seem to be working. I turn the thermostat but no heat flows through. It would probably be a simple matter putting it right, if one knew what one was doing. I've passed the caretaker several times without asking for help.

In order to stay warm, you sleep in a foetal position. You're wrapped in a semi-thick blanket, often dressed in a long-armed hoodie.

I sleep in the room next door, in a double bed. It's pitch black in there at night, and the fluffy duvet keeps the cold at bay.

I keep ordering you to do meaningless tasks. Every morning I tell you to fold up the blanket and leave it piled on the armrest of the sofa, with your pillow on top. I tell you that it's important for us to keep some order in the apartment, and that you must do this both for the sake of having some cosiness but also good hygiene. But the actual reason is something quite different. When I see the pile of bed linen it feels as if it belongs to a house guest, a visitor. And my hope is that you'll look at it in the same way.

Do you?

When you prepare your sleeping spot in the evenings and put your things away in the mornings, does it strike you that this is not your home, you're only here temporarily and at my say-so?

In my darkest moments I'm convinced that this is all premeditated. I think to myself that your intention must have been to take possession of my home, exploit my generosity and goodness. That our deal about you coming here once per week was only a pretext to push me out altogether.

You're making yourself worryingly at home. You move unselfconsciously between the rooms, filling them with your presence and your smells. You burp, fart, shit and pee without closing the toilet door behind you. You forget to flush and can't be bothered to wash your hands, then you walk around touching things, touching me. On a number of occasions I've sat down on splashes of urine because you don't lift the toilet seat. When you pee, you don't direct the jet against the inside of the toilet bowl, instead you bring it down directly into the water, so that the noise resounds throughout the flat, penetrating into my inside ear. It's more of a rule than an exception that when I lift the toilet lid, I see globules of stuck-on shit, solidified into crustaceous deposits on the white porcelain – you've not bothered to scrub off these lumps, and so, consumed with rage, I'm forced to battle them with the toilet brush. If you're at home, I immediately send you to do it yourself. But just as often I get onto my knees and start scrubbing.

Last Saturday you accidentally knocked my hard drive so that it fell to the floor, erasing seven years of documented memories in a millisecond.

You never thank me for the food when we go out to eat. I invite you to two or three meals per day. A part of me thinks it's healthy. You don't feel the need to be polite, which indicates that you are secure and that you can be yourself. Another part of me finds you ungrateful and spoiled.

After you've eaten you never put away your crockery in the dishwasher. You don't wipe away cornflakes or bread-crumbs from the table. You leave the cheese, jam and butter out, so that they dry out or go mouldy and have to be thrown away.

Never, not one single time, have you helped me clean the flat. You don't do laundry either. I've tried to make you. I've said it's your turn to sort the dirty laundry into laundry bags, so that I can take them down to the cellar. But separating white T-shirts from coloured – you can't even manage that.

You borrow my things without asking. Sometimes I look at you and think to myself that something has changed – did you have a haircut, have you grown by a centimetre or two? No, actually you've just gone through my wardrobe. You're walking around in my tracksuit top, jacket, hat, my underpants. Clamped around your head I see the headphones I've been looking for. You don't say anything. You don't think it might be interpreted as impudent or lacking respect. You are impersonating me and everything is absolutely in order.

After practice you forget your sweat-soaked clothes and your wet towel in the sports bag. Twenty-four hours later there's a rotten smell in the flat.

The worst thing of all is your noisy chomping. It sends me into a panic. Shivers run through my body. You eat with your mouth wide open. You slurp, guzzle, smack your lips. I tell you to stop. 'Close your mouth when you're eating, bro.' You close your mouth, grinning. Then you forget what I just said and you go on guzzling. Sometimes I chew you out or I get up in protest and sit at another table. It hurts your feelings, but if we're going to live together, you have to learn to eat like a regular person.

17

Flaming blue light spreads through the room. I've just taken a nap and now I vacantly watch the trembling, eerie glow moving in circles overhead, down the wall and across the floor. I see its intensity picking up, and it seems to widen just as it creeps onto me and crosses over me. Only then do I react. I make a thrashing movement which is so abrupt I end up on the edge of the sofa, and then fall hard against the floor.

Three police cars are parked on the other side of the street, their blue lights soundlessly rotating. Four policemen are standing by the gate, and two are walking inside the building through an open door. A police radio crackles, a shrill voice cuts through the air. I don't know what it's saying, but I do know what's being said. My colleague Carlos called me in the night and told me that a kid he's the contact person for was involved in yesterday's shooting. Two young men were hit, one in the foot and the other in the thigh. As the police would have it, it was attempted murder. But according to Carlos it was a warning. He said that the kid had probably taken refuge with his uncle, who lives in the house opposite ours.

*　*　*

The sun goes behind a cloud and a light rain falls. You manage the feat of three people balancing on a rickety full-size bicycle. Abbe steers and pedals, Josef sits on the parcel rack with his hands on Abbe's shoulders, and you are on the handlebars with your arms stretched out on either side.

You laugh until you're choking.

You yell: 'Jack, I'm flying!'

Abbe answers: 'I'll never let go, Jack! I'll never let go!'

Then suddenly Abbe loses control of the handlebars and you hurtle down the hill at high speed. I cycle after you, pedalling as hard as I can. And when I catch up with you, you're all lying in a pile in the grass, doubled up with laughter.

We're on our way to Lindängen. I for a reading by the author Kristian Lundberg, you to play basketball outside the library. The local authority has put up two baskets on the paved area, and I can see you through the window as I take a seat on a chair.

Lundberg shuffles onto the stage. He looks worn out, as if he hasn't had any sleep since the nineties.

I'm the only man among the audience of twenty-three. The only one who hasn't turned forty.

I feel uncomfortable, think about legging it out of there. But I'm worried that he might see me if I get up.

My tense nerves have to do with intimacy. Or ambivalence, rather. It's almost shocking to see him in real life. I've read most of the things he's written. I feel a sort of kinship with him. But every time his apathetic eyes sweep over the room,

I blush and sink into my chair. Lundberg and Dagerman. How many hours have I not spent with them both?

Especially Dagerman. He's the house god. The unrivalled master of Swedish literature. He punctured the membrane between life and literature, gave form to an acute sense of awareness, wrote as if everything was at stake. Lundberg is more flesh and blood. He writes with dignity about contemporary life. And he's uncorrupted. Humble and confounded by the shift that has taken place. It's as if a trapdoor has opened in Swedish society, and a new underclass has emerged. Lundberg tries to position himself and understand, but mostly he is just agonized and perplexed.

Dagerman is still as relevant. In the short story *To Kill a Child*, from 1948, he is writing about our current situation, about young people dying. More tangibly: how our innocence – our naivety – has made us into monsters. A young couple are driving their car down a country road, it's a sunny day. A boy walks out of his home to go and fetch sugar for his parents. We follow the sequence of events. Already in advance we know – I mean, already in the title it's clear – that the child is going to die. We understand *how* his death will happen, and therefore also what needs to be done to prevent it. It makes for horrendous reading. The disaster is beyond recall, even before it has taken place. The boy dies, crushed against the gleaming bumper which is dented and red-stained by his blood. The unease lingers for a long time. Yes, it has stayed with me ever since I saw the short film at school, and whenever I have read the short story over the years. We know that the kids are going to die. We understand why they die, how they're going to die, but we don't do enough to prevent it happening.

The clouds scatter and the sun breaks out. I look out of the window and, at that very moment, Josef falls badly and grazes his knee. Lundberg gets asked a question by the moderator: 'How would you like to be remembered?' Josef stays sitting down on the asphalt, his face between his knees to hide the fact that he's crying. Lundberg grunts, crosses his arms, breathes heavily through his nose. You and Abbe sit on the ground at Josef's side. You pat him on the back, and Abbe unscrews the lid of his water bottle. Lundberg says something about how he has more books inside of him. It's a proper flesh wound. Josef's face glistens with tears. Abbe says something and kisses his hair. He hugs him, you both hug him, you embrace your friend. Then Abbe up-ends the water bottle and rinses off Josef's wound.

18

I'm storing a mattress in my attic space; it has stayed with me through the years every time I've moved. The mattress is grubby. The pale, thinning fabric is stained. And at one end there's a tear, through which the foam-rubber burgeons. When I last moved, the mattress was unintentionally left outside in the rain. It got soaked, so that I had to put it out to dry in the laundry overnight. The damp led to an attack of vermin; wingless creepie-crawlies ate their way into the foam-rubber and nestled into the seams of the mattress cover. For a week I woke every night after scratching my skin to shreds, my legs and body aflame with blood-red and pink blotches. At first, I didn't know what was eating me. When I inspected the fabric I saw no trace of anything. But then I noticed little colonies of blindly moving insects. I rolled up the mattress and fixed it with silver tape, carried it up to the attic, and slept on the sofa until I could afford to buy a bed.

The mattress has no sentimental value. I keep it as an insurance policy against the fear of suddenly losing everything and having to use it once more.

* * *

The first time I slept on the mattress was soon after my mother died. I was nineteen. In addition to my mother being the only person I had confided in, she had also administered my whole life and navigated through the bureaucracy that I didn't even know was surrounding us. When Mum died I had no idea of how to be an adult.

I knew nothing about waiting lists for public housing, had no contacts in the illegal housing market. I could not take a loan to buy myself a home – did not know one could take a loan to buy your own place to live, didn't even know one could own a home. I didn't know shelters existed. In other words, I fell straight through the coarse mesh of the social safety net. I wasn't young enough to get the support I needed, not mature or socially adjusted to the extent of knowing where to turn, or what rights I had. I remember that I called the city's local authority property company, after a tip-off by a friend. The woman's voice addressing me turned me mute with horror. She seemed to have been pre-recorded, her exhortations were impossible to understand. I hung up with a feeling of being unclean.

I couldn't have known then what I know now. Sweden is a thoroughly institutionalized country, whose rules and prescriptions, queueing systems and forms, opening hours and social norms, telephone answering systems and mechanical people create a system into which one must more or less be born and raised, in order to have an overall perspective of, or understand, or be able to make use of it. If one is a recent arrival into the country or uneducated as I was then, and does not understand the mumbo jumbo, the jargon, the cryptography, or have contacts to guide one through the thorny obstacles, or an ability to anticipate where the pitfalls lie and how to exploit the failings and grey zones of the system, then one ends up excluded. I ended up excluded. I fell between the paragraphs. My brother and I were forced to let go of the flat after my mother's death. My brother moved in with a friend. I ended up with some friends of my mother, in the countryside. After that I was invited to live with Hamid's family for a while.

Hamid rolled out a mattress on the floor in his childhood bedroom, but he let me have the bed. 'It's good for my back to lie on the floor,' I remember him saying. He lied for my sake, but I didn't protest.

I was an awful guest at Hamid's family home. I ate their food, never did any cleaning, offered nothing in return for their sacrifice. I don't even remember thanking them when, a couple of months later, I felt compelled to move on.

We said our farewell from the front door. Hamid had stuffed the mattress into a black bin bag. He insisted that I had to take it with me. I hugged him, I took the mattress and my bag, and then left.

After those months at Hamid's, all my available possibilities of accommodation had been exhausted. It was winter. I found my way back to my old middle school, which was in the midst of building works and temporarily emptied of students. I recalled that the caretaker there had been a generous-spirited person, and I felt she might understand me. My plan was to plead with her to let me sleep there until I was back on my feet.

The cold clawed at my face. For two hours I waited outside the school, until finally she swung into the car park. She remembered me, and I got straight to the point. I told her I was homeless and an orphan. I lied about having contacts and a flat on the go, to which I'd gain entry in a week or so. If I could just use one of the classrooms for a little while, everything would be fine after that.

The physics classroom was best suited for the purpose. It lay at the far end of the building and faced onto a small clump of trees, almost completely hidden from sight from the outside. No one would know that I was there.

The caretaker looked at me. Her face was inscrutable. She turned around and headed towards the entrance, while muttering: 'We should be able to manage that.'

Every morning I rolled up the mattress and put it next to an empty glass cabinet, and every evening I rolled it out on the cold linoleum floor.

This is rock bottom, I thought, staring up at the fluorescent tubes. *You can't get any lower than this.* Those weeks in the physics classroom were the loneliest weeks of my life. I didn't talk to anyone. I lived as if I'd tumbled into a crack in the world.

Shortly after, a friend fixed a sub-lease for me on a place on the outskirts of town. And a few years later I was able to buy my first flat, thanks to my boss at that time, who vouched for me and advanced the entire deposit. The mattress accompanied me.

It's still up there in the attic, stowed away. It was left there because I thought it might come in handy once more.

Which was quite right. Because now you're here. And you're where I was once – rock bottom.

So I'll carry the mattress down from the attic; inspect it for vermin. And then move your sheet over from the sofa.

19

On one of the rare occasions when my mother commented on the powers that be – meaning the social elite, which included the top echelons of the working class and up – she said that they both wanted and did not want our fury. I understand what she meant. Fury, given expression in forms such as cursing, yelling, violence and rioting, is regarded as the standard means of communication of uncivilized people, and it becomes an affirmation of the good sense of our subordination: we're primitive and therefore unworthy of a higher position.

Anger is also desirable because it's expressive, visible, easy to propagate and mobilize against, and put down. An example of this might be that if I put up any resistance to the police's abuse of power, then as a result I'll take a beating. Another example: the flaring gang conflicts in *blatte* areas. Nothing is more useful to sneering far-right or racist parties than the murdering ways of *blattes*. The gangs have no real power. Their violence is focused primarily on other *blattes* in the places where the underclasses live. There's no threat to the social order. The violence actually helps to cement it.

It's an altogether different matter when it comes to *political* fury, the righteous hatred of injustice channelled into the fight for social change. This, I like to think, is what my mother meant when she spoke of unwanted fury.

A while back I worked at an event for young people in Herrgården in Rosengård, an area whose vulnerability is unprecedented in Sweden. In Herrgården, over half the children live in poverty and the rate of unemployment is the highest in the entire country. Before the event kicked off, with the tents already put up, the bouncy castles inflated and my colleagues all gone off to have their lunch, I sat down on a bench in the sun with a book in my hand.

Only a few metres away, the Rosengård riots had flared up in the winter of 2008 in an insignificant cellar, whose windows were covered, as if it had no particular use. The property company that owned the premises had, for reasons that were unclear, evicted the Muslim association that had been renting it. Youths forced their way inside and occupied it, which was when the riots kicked off.

For weeks, people took to the streets. They came from near and far to vandalize and to attack the police with stones, bangers and improvised bombs. Cars, schools, petrol stations, stairwells and containers were set alight. The whole area was cooking. There were hundreds of police in or around Rosengård. I was also there with my colleagues. We were mediating and trying to calm down the atmosphere, talking to young people and the police. I felt sympathetic to those who had started the riots. Felt enlivened by the hemmed-in anger spending itself in fire. But local people took a sore hit. And when the headlines were cabled out in the world's media, and the authorities made use of their military expertise and training, and the politicians poured on their lighter fuel, it was hard to see any meaning to it all. With the exception, obviously, of the fact that the Swedish people had now acquainted themselves with the full force of the fury of the underclass.

As I sat on that bench, I read a biography of the writer Harry Martinson, born in the early 1900s, orphaned at an early age and sold at auction. Before his writing career took off, he worked as a seaman or was, at various times, a tramp. He was awarded the Nobel Prize in Literature. Four years later, committed to a mental hospital, he slit his stomach open with a pair of scissors and died in terrible agony. The feeling of homelessness haunted Martinson throughout his life and is described in his books. Martinson was filled with hatred. And the more I read about him and the books he wrote, the more convinced I am that it was precisely this hatred, and his inability to handle it, that took his life.

Poverty is not the worst because it hounds a person to
death
because she does not wish to walk the path of life in shoes
that are too small.
Poverty is the worst because of the inner hatred it creates,
an endless battle of pinpricks which
kills with more certainty than anything else in houses of
poverty,

when a human being no longer knows what's for the
   best
because she no longer even notices the wind or the
   sun.

It struck me that the kids in Herrgården are the poor
orphans of our new age. The class system rots the teeth
in their jaws, tears them out of the hands of their parents,
forces them to live with cockroaches and rats in the mould-
damaged, cramped flats of slum lords.

Once the event kicked off, children from all over Rosengård
took part. I remember thinking to myself: the thing that had
taken Martinson's life was what was also sucking the essence
out of the young people who were here. The very same ones
who, with peals of laughter, were running between the bouncy
castle and the sprinkler, dancing, eating hot dogs and being
face-painted.

*Poverty was the worst, because of the inner hatred it creates,
an endless battle of pinpricks.* It would kill them more surely
than anything else in the crumbling high-rise blocks.

My mother never cultivated her hatred; never used it as a
catalyst for liberation or political struggle. She did the same
as all the other adults I knew: quelled her feelings, denied
them, and forgot.

Mum was satisfied with a sort of emotional neutrality. The
absence of unhappiness. Nothing grand. Peaceful walks with
the dog. Coffee, cigarettes. Books. Knowing that her sons
were not dead. Break even.

Mum preferred not to interact with other people. Reluctantly, and with her nerves on edge, she took part in parents' evenings and academic reviews with teachers. She dissimulated. Put on a mask. Smiled and nodded politely, vibrating with restlessness. I hated seeing her like that.

I had a feeling that she was afraid of being exposed. As if she was harbouring a secret – the secret of herself, her innermost being – which the masters saw through just by looking at her.

Mum never saw me play basketball. The unpleasantness of having to small-talk with the parents of my teammates and the trainers that were in charge of me, in addition to her disinterest when it came to sport, kept her well away. I was no kiddy player. I made my way into the elite. I was ranked as one of the best players in the country in my age group. I was mentioned in the newspapers. But she never came to my games. This made me sad.

I remember her telephone calls with the bank. My stomach bunched up when I heard her trying at the same time to be dignified and desperate, in order to win sympathy and mercy while she accounted for her difficulties in supporting her family.

Some time back I went through old files I'd stored in the attic and I found my mother's tax returns. They confirmed my understanding of the situation. After the rent, bills, loan instalments and other fixed costs were paid off, only about a thousand kronor remained. That financial equation was an impossibility, and any unforeseen costs, even the most trivial sum, could make her fall apart. As a result, I didn't like to tell her when my basketball shoes had split along a seam, or when we were going on tour and had to pay the membership fee, or when I needed money for the bus fare. Instead, I just stole or found other ways of protecting her from having to pay.

Our life was stripped back. We rarely did anything together that came at a cost. No holidays, no cinema, no excursions, no restaurants, no trips to Denmark or other cities around. Despite her difficulties, Mum rarely turned to the social institutions that had been created exactly for people like her.

My friends' dirt-poor parents had exactly the same approach. For a while, Hamid's mother worked as a baker in a small bakery. Her payment: as much bread as she could carry. I remember how worked up we got when she came in from work with bags of bread, rolls, doughnuts and sugared buns with vanilla cream. Until I realized that this was a form of slavery. Her clarification was: 'I can't find a job, I can't just walk around the apartment all day.'

We – the children – were well aware that in a social and economic sense we were on a lower rung. For reasons that were inscrutable we were expected to be grateful, keep a low profile and be submissive. We were indebted to society because we were a drain on its resources, and therefore we had no right to complain. I didn't understand how all this was constituted. Most of us lived our lives on the margins – there were no resources left to drain. Besides, my friends' parents and my mother were among the hardest-working, least likely to complain, most sick and ravaged, and in many cases most honest people that I ever met. They never demanded their rights – stupidly, because society was pissing on them.

20

When you look at me, Elijah, what do you see?

When I laugh, when I'm serious, distant, grumpy, happy, indifferent, boastful, jocular, reserved, mean, do you sense my anxiety?

My face in your presence rarely gives expression to strong feelings. There are never aggressive shrieks or streaks of tears. There's no uncontrolled laughter. My face doesn't darken with anger or shout or sing for joy or rest in harmony. When you look at my face, Elijah, do you see my anguish?

No. You don't.

You don't see shit.

If there's one thing I manage to do well, it's the hiding of my feelings and thoughts. The person I am. The human that you don't know.

If I asked you what my mother's name was, whether she was alive, if I had siblings, from what country my parents came, how old I am, what my experience was of primary school and secondary school, what my childhood was like, when I was last in love, who had broken my heart, where my father was, what films, artists or books had been important to me, you would not be able to give me any answers.

You are unaware of the most important aspects of my life.

I, on the other hand, know masses about you. Obviously I am not in a position to know about your life before we first had contact. But I do know that your father comes from Trinidad and Tobago and Grenada, and your mother from Sweden and Denmark. I know that you have two half-siblings, an adult brother in the USA and an adult sister in Sweden. You listen to the same sort of music as I once did – New York hip hop. You have never read a book. You like Denzel Washington movies. You were in love with a girl while you were in primary school, you kissed one another, nothing else happened, you are thinking of getting back in contact and asking her if she wants to go out with you. You perceive your growing up in Nydala and your schooling as difficult, threatening, fun, insecure and boring.

From your ongoing childhood I have hundreds – thousands – of memories. And I am capable of explaining – perhaps with even more exactitude than you could manage yourself – how you are as a person, how you have lived, what stands out about you and why. I can put words to it, I can contextualize. And I can use it against you if I want to. I can account for incidents you have forgotten about, for hilarities and embarrassments and dangers you don't understand or remember that you were exposed to. I can exaggerate or lie about tendencies in you which are rather undesirable. I can inflate them, and say that you were a nasty, or tearful, or weak child. I can make things up about you, which you can't deny because you don't even remember them, because they never actually happened. I can compose a picture of you that's false. I can say things about you with such conviction, and repeat them so endlessly, that you'll take them as literal truth. I can break you down; damage your self-esteem, make you loathe yourself. In many respects I know you better than you know yourself. The immediate, corporeal and sensory experience of being Elijah is obviously something you are more intimate with yourself – after all, you live with yourself. But I have at my disposal an overview of your life and person, a greater understanding of who you are. Given that I'm a grown-up, I'm more experienced than you, craftier and more calculating, with a greater capacity for analysis and reflection, as well as better equipped with general knowledge and social understanding. You, on the other hand, are more driven by your emotions. More intuitive, impulsive, passionate and emotional. Therefore your life, at least when reckoned using my yardstick, is richer, more open, more shot through with light, than my own. And maybe this is the reason why I nurture you as I do.

That is only partly true. But if I were to explain to an outsider, let's say one of my friends, why you are here, it's the reason I would offer. Feed the light to oppose the darkness.

To my friends I would say that I had to dig deep before I made the decision to take care of you. That I let you move in even though I felt an extreme reluctance, and I'd have to forgo my own comfort. My friends would be impressed. They'd say I'm a good man, there ought to be more people like me, that I have acted with generosity.

I wouldn't tell my friends that my feelings for you can be so contradictory, that in one moment I have to try extremely hard just to put up with your presence and hold back my aggressions, only in the next moment to be overwhelmed by such a tenderness for you that without any doubt I could kill anyone who harmed you. That I am in a crisis that most simply could be described as a constant, increasing, acute need to patch something together, save something, keep something intact.

I wouldn't tell them that, to avoid the pain caused by the loss of you, I do my utmost to reduce your significance and your value as a human being.

I wouldn't tell them that I have developed strategies to protect myself against this loss and pre-empt your disappearance. And that I often, sometimes many times per day, imagine the disaster unfolding – I visualize how you suddenly grow cold and repudiating, until I confront you about this, and you answer that I have always been false to you, always been manipulative and controlling. And that you never want to see me again.

I fantasize about how you are sucked into drug addiction, and how you quickly go into a spiral of dependence and I have to cut our contact, forget you.

I fantasize about you being drawn into the gangs, coming into contact with older criminals whose influence on you is greater than mine.

I fantasize about your violent death. Inside my head, I watch how someone shoots and kills you in the street, how you are executed outside the sports hall or massacred in the passenger seat of some car, or beaten to death, or stabbed in the belly until you bleed to death.

These, and thousands of other horrific scenarios, pass through my inner visions. I torment myself with them. Steel myself. One disaster is worse than the next. And none of this is far beyond the realms of possibility. All are, in fact, quite logical endings to your young, chaotic life.

There were similar patterns in my own childhood. I was abandoned by people close to me and I developed ways of protecting myself from losses. I visualized them. Played them like films in my brain, to anticipate them, accept them, and soften the trauma.

In my imagination, my mother died and left me and was raped a thousand times.

If she stayed out with the dog for more than an hour, I saw before me how she lay murdered in a bush. If she sat deep in thought for too long, I would sometimes experience a sense of panic, and my feeling would be, 'Come out of there, Mum, you mustn't stay in there!' And if she didn't come home from the supermarket after half an hour, I thought she'd met a man and run off with him. Sometimes my despair was so overwhelming that I began to dissolve at the edges. I made plans for a life of loneliness without my mother, for how I had to make a living, how I must tell my teacher I wouldn't be coming back to school.

It was obsessive. I was haunted by the thought. My mother would be taken from me. It was only a matter of time.

I knew it.

And I was right.

One evening my grandfather called and asked if I had spoken to Mum. She was at the hospital to do some tests because of what she had described as unusual fatigue and constant pains.

'Spoken to her about what?' I asked.

'About the cancer,' he blurted out. 'Your mother has cancer.'

Mum had told her father to keep it to himself. She had called him as soon as she got the diagnosis, and she told him they'd found several tumours. Lung cancer. It had spread throughout her body. It was too late. She was going to die. But he mustn't say anything to the children.

Shocked by it all, he couldn't hold it in. He sounded dry and reasonable on the telephone. If there was any sense of devastation, no trace of it could be heard in his rasping voice. 'Your mother has cancer.'

'No,' I said, not fully taking in what he'd just told me. 'That can't be right. She's just tired. It's tiredness and pain.'

'No,' he said. 'It's cancer. I just spoke to her. And it's spread too.'

'But that can't be right,' I insisted, while the realization slowly began to sink in. 'It's not right.'

'Yes,' he said. 'Unfortunately it is. You might as well go and see her.'

I handed the receiver to my brother. Then I ran into the bedroom, yelling: 'I knew it! I knew it! I knew it!'

I threw myself on the bed and, for the last time, I prayed to that god I did not believe in.

'I knew it! I knew it!'

I had always known it.

* * *

89

How a heart is broken is irrelevant. Whether a person's disappearance is caused by that person dying in an accident or taking their own life, or being murdered, or falling sick, or leaving by their own volition, or being caught up in drug addiction – when all is said and done, it is an irrelevance to the heart.

By means of rationality, one can differentiate between the different kinds of partings, and understand them as involuntary, self-inflicted or planned. And the immediate emotional response – panic, shock, anger, emptiness, despair, indignation – may vary. But the lasting thing, the consistent core of experience, the lesson extracted, is the sense of abandonment.

One has been left. Someone who you belonged with has been taken away, taken from you, has let you down.

That is the only thing you know.

The only thing the heart knows.

21

Snow whirled over St Johannesplan. We passed the church. The homeless people's tarpaulins were dressed in white. I had time to think: *Are they still alive in there? How do they keep warm? Are there corpses under layered blankets, frozen stiff?*

Last autumn I cycled past the church entrance and saw a woman priest driving away a beggar from the front steps. The sight of it shook me up. The beggar had sat down shortly before a service or baptism; he must have thought he had a good chance of getting a few coins together. Not so. The priest came storming out of the heavy door. Her cassock fluttered in the wind as she saw off the godless wretch.

I had told you to spend Christmas at home with your mother. It came as a surprise to you. But you'd been missing her, and you didn't give me any lip about it.

Stepping into the warmth of the make-up shop on Triangeln to find a present for her, we walked around, unsure of ourselves. 'Mum would like this,' you said several times, pointing at products you knew nothing about. 'This one's nice, Nick, she'd be really happy if she got that.'

In the end, I called over the sales assistant. She asked a couple of questions about your mother and what she was like as a person. 'Does she have any special hobby? Is she quiet or active?'

You said that she was kind and giggly.

We walked out of there with you proudly carrying a crimson package containing two bottles of shampoo and a tube of hair oil. It cost me 298 smackers.

The sun set at three. I walked you to the bus stop, hugged you, wished you a merry Christmas. Then ambled home and sat in the kitchen with a coffee.

On the rooftop opposite sat a rook in its gleaming black suit, shaking some powdery snow from its feathers and sliding its beak along the gutter. In the window down and across, in the flat where the fat man with a large flatscreen TV often watched porn, there were children running about. Lit candles flickered along the windowsill.

In the shoot-up park, snowflakes glistened from within the deepening gloom. Black clouds, though slightly lighter than the background of the sky, glided slow and spirit-like over the rooftops. A bit further away, next to the church, two cranes rose through the mist. They had stood immobile like that for over a month. Their noses were turned towards the church steeple, whose clock had stopped.

I have been on my own for four of the last twelve Christmases.

Every Christmas for the last six years I've kept notes about the day and how it has gone. It doesn't make for very cheerful reading. I hardly talk to anyone. I take long walks, sit in restaurants, read, watch TV.

During a few of those Christmases I've made the following

note: *No one has called. No one has wished me Merry Christmas.*

Lonely people are well advised to settle in Möllan, Malmö. Whatever day it is, many restaurants and local shops are open. Many residents and business owners are Muslims. I celebrate with them in secret.

Christmas is the high festival of self-pity. The fact that I have no plans, that I can go outside into the chill, passing flats in which families have gathered, stare at them, move on to the next window, have another stare while thinking about how no one is missing me or waiting for me to arrive, arouses contradictory feelings. Or, in fact, not contradictory. It creates a void, a possibility. I can make a choice for myself about how I should feel. I can focus on no one being able to make any claims on me, I'm on my own, unsought, or I can be sentimental, get out photographs from the Christmases of my childhood, myself, Mum and my brother, and make myself melancholic or gloomy or unfathomably tragic. Or else I can persuade myself that it isn't so damn terrible. Because it just isn't.

At five o'clock I had dinner at Kebab Time. A Kurdish group was celebrating some festivity, though not Christmas. Among them I caught sight of Maria, who came forward to say hello. Her daughter, whose father is Ghanaian, looked like an angel in her white dress with puff shoulders and a glittering tiara. As I looked at the luminous girl, it struck me that I had probably never thought of Black girls as angels. The pictures of angels that I've been fed are white cherubs with chubby cheeks, Christian depictions of girls with golden locks, or young white women in American films. 'You're looking so lovely, just like a little angel,' I said to Maria's daughter. She smiled, her mouth full of French fries.

Back home I took a bath, soaked myself for over an hour. I read two chapters from Arundhati Roy's novel, *The God of Small Things*. Felt low. Switched to *Nadirs* by Herta Müller, who, with her Eastern-bloc aura and dignified, heavy-going, chainsmoker look, reminds me of my mother.

At eight o'clock you came home. You seemed down, but I didn't ask why. Instead, I went into the kitchen and heated some chocolate milk in the microwave and poured some nuts and raisins into a bowl. I brought two lit candles into the living room and put them down on the windowsill.

You chuckled when you saw me. 'What's with those?'

Wrapped in a plaid blanket each, with the starless sky like a black sea outside the windows, we munched nuts and watched the second half of *Independence Day*.

When the credits were rolling, you said, with satisfaction: 'This has got to be the life, Nick, right? This is the way you do it. Hey, could you fix my razor lines, Nick? I wanna be fresh tomorrow.'

'No problem,' I said. 'What's happening tomorrow?'

'Nothin' special. But you never know. Hey, I could meet the love of my life. I gotta look the part.'

22

We were there to buy milk, soap and Cocoa Puffs, and we crisscrossed between the aisles at Lidl. It must have been our aimless wandering, our messing about, the fact that you had your hood drawn up over your head, and our being *blattes*, that made the shop assistant suspicious. At first his glances weren't very noticeable. Then, he started padding along behind us, and then finally he stood in front of us with his hands on his hips as if he wanted a fight. You flinched as he stepped into your field of vision. I was also caught off guard. We stood there in silence, looking at one another. He was a tall man. Maybe six foot three. In a loud voice, so that other people would be able to hear, I said: 'You see this dude here, Elijah? He's a racist, that's why he's following us, because he thinks we're going to steal something.'

The shop assistant's face turned red. 'I'm calling the police,' he exclaimed in a surprisingly high tone of voice. 'If you don't leave, I'll call the police.'

'You do that. Call the police,' I answered, putting my hand on your shoulder and ushering you along towards the checkouts.

On our way out, other customers were looking at us. Three or four people stood silently in the queue, stiff as mannequins. I put the shopping basket with the soap and the milk on the floor. A woman with a cloth bag snatched up her carton of milk from the conveyor belt; petrified, smiling.

'Fucking moron,' I said without turning around. We walked out of Lidl.

On the way home you went on and on: 'What a racist. Honest, Nick, what a fucking racist.'

'Yeah,' I said. 'But screw him. Let's buy what we need at Hemköp instead.'

For probably half an hour afterwards I felt tremors through my body. Partly from the adrenaline and the anger welling up with nowhere to go. Partly out of fear of what might have happened if I'd thrown a punch at that sales assistant.

It's a new experience. I'm no longer just responsible for myself. In any situation we find ourselves in, especially if there's some potential danger, I have to have consideration for you and your safety. That sales assistant was too big for me to handle. In other words, it's easy to imagine a scenario in which he gets me into a bad position, down on the floor, and then you fly at him in an attempt to come to my aid.

I would then be exposing you to danger. Or actually, I *did* expose you to danger by provoking him and letting myself be provoked. The thought of it is unbearable. It makes me remember an incident in my childhood, when my brother was brought down by a bigger, stronger guy. My brother was standing by a stone wall, messing around with a ball. I was on the grass, about ten metres away. Out of nowhere an unknown guy showed up, pushed my brother over, squatted on top of him, and started feeding punches into his face. Everything went black for me. In a panic I ran up to the guy, jumped onto his back, yelling at the top of my voice while pummelling the side of his head. He flinched, no more than a slight movement; but I was thrown off and landed on my stomach, grazing my chin against the asphalt. At that same moment my brother managed to work himself free. He got out a retractable knife from his pocket, quickly opening the blade. The guy reacted by moving his hands around, instinctively shielding himself. My brother slashed him. Put a gash in his hand. The blood went flying. The guy withdrew. He held up his hand in front of his face before turning around and running.

23

One night during the Malmö Festival there was a tumult when two police officers grabbed hold of a boy, threw him down on the ground and twisted his shoulder out of joint. I was working that evening, was one of the few adults in that compact circle of youths who saw the boy assaulted.

The assault was premeditated but it was not preceded by any conflict or confrontation. It was not some outlet for hatred or blind rage, retaliation or sadistic pleasure. No feelings could be deduced in the police officers' faces. The men had followed the boy and his friends from Stortorget through the surging crowd and had waited for the moment when he was in the bicycle lane – the street where there were more people than anywhere else, where the assault would attract the most attention and generate the most fear – before they went for him.

The attack was synchronized. Without even looking at each other or exchanging a single word, as if they formed a single body, they knocked the boy to the ground with a sweeping movement. The man who had tripped the boy up pressed one of his knees against his backside and the other over his thigh, at the same time as he grasped the boy's feet and bent them back. The other man twisted the boy's arms and locked them in a hold over his back, pressed his knee against the boy's neck and then turned his gaze towards us. Like a hunter, triumphant, with his foot on his prey.

I was standing two metres in front of him. He looked at me but he didn't see me, didn't see anyone. Then, he twisted the boy's shoulder out of joint. I heard the crunching sound, and now when I think about it, it must have transmitted into those men's bodies; although I didn't see the slightest sign of it in their faces, they must have felt the quivering motion as the child's arm, up until that point held in a tensile position, was transformed in a moment into an armless sleeve.

When one human being strikes another human being in anger, it's comprehensible. When one human being strikes another human being for the sake of hatred, it's comprehensible. But when one human being strikes another without feeling anything at all he's no longer a human, but a beast.

This blind, curious violence is described in the autobiography *If This is a Man* by the writer and chemist Primo Levi. Levi has been captured by German SS men and is just about to be loaded into a goods train to be taken to an extermination camp when this violence is visited upon him:

> Here we received the first blows: and it was so new and senseless that we felt no pain, neither in body nor in spirit. Only a profound amazement: how can one hit a man without anger?

More police turned up and roughly bundled their way through the crowd, forming a ring around the child and the men, while gesturing and shouting. Bodies around me shoved and pushed. Voices rose up, increasingly loud and angry. You were standing right next to me. Intently you stared at what was happening there on the ground, but you didn't raise your voice with all the others. Then you turned to me. Your gaze was neither pleading nor judgemental. Only then did I become aware of myself. Up until that point I had been a part of the audience, an observer of the spectacle. Now that you were looking at me, it was as if the situation became real. A number of feelings came over me at the same time. I was afraid that you and the other kids would see me and that your disappointment about my inaction, my not trying to save the boy, would force me to reluctantly step forward only to be wrestled to the ground myself. My shame turned into a touchiness and irritation about the men not noticing me; to them I wasn't an adult, merely one of a mass of youths; they expected nothing of me and my presence was irrelevant. At the same time, I took their nonchalance as a sort of provocation, as if they were checking whether I'd dare to defy them and try to help the child, so that they could mete out the same treatment to me.

It was also striking that I felt almost no empathy with the boy who'd been physically assaulted. I couldn't see him as a person, a child who'd been subjected to violence. Because doing so would give me a guilty conscience. Who in that case was I, then, if I was just an observer? Could I even be held accountable? When he cried out in pain and panic, one part of me just wished he'd be quiet. Sure, he was entitled to feel some pain, there was no problem about that, but not so much pain that it ended up stirring the anger and frustration of the crowd, which would force me to get involved and run the risk of being put in his position.

When the men were done, they carried the boy over to a police van, which had been driven onto the pavement on the other side of the bridge. They moved at a brisk pace, carrying him as you'd carry a rolled-up rug, while the other men kept back a chastened-looking group of youths who stayed on their tails.

I went back to work, relieved that it was all over but also worried that you or someone else had lost respect for me; I pondered on how I might win it back.

Maybe this was the balance I was trying to restore when I confronted that man in the aisles of Lidl. I only understood this afterwards. I had stood up to the shop assistant, I had put my foot down. I'm sure that you thought I'd acted like a man of principle; even though it had all been a show for the gallery.

24

Yesterday afternoon you sent a text message to my telephone: **Get this, Nick, I'm fucking driving!** And in the photo that followed, you were shown sitting at the wheel of a car.

I looked at it for a long time without understanding what I was seeing.

You're fourteen years old, driving what I assume is a stolen car at sixty, eighty, a hundred kilometres an hour down a main road. You asked Abbe in the passenger seat to take a picture of you so that you could send it to me.

You look grim. You stare straight ahead and you've sucked in your lower lip, the way you do when you're concentrating. The road you're hurtling down and the roadside, which can be seen outside the window, are blurred because of the high speed. The sky in the background has dissolved into white and turquoise. You're spinning the wheel as if you're about to make a turn. If it weren't for the fact that the photo was sent after the event, meaning that I knew for a fact that you'd survived it, I'd guess at that very moment you were about to skid off the road. The steering wheel is about 90 degrees to one side, as if you're swerving or have noticed too late a bend coming up in the road.

You didn't crash into a rock wall or frontally collide with an oncoming vehicle. You survived and you sent me the pictorial evidence.

When I received the message I felt neither angry nor frightened. I didn't think to myself that I could have lost you for ever. But I did think you were an idiot, without attaching any particular emphasis to those words. And I had time to reflect on how this was the sort of behaviour that I expected of you, the sort of thing you expose yourself to – and me. It never occurred to me that in that one moment you could have died.

I felt mortified. Is this how you see me? As one of your buddies? Someone who'd be impressed by this kind of crap? What sort of impression had I made on you, if you thought suicide games would earn my respect? What the hell does this say about me?

You have wounded my ego. Made me feel stupid.

Is this the way you want it, Elijah? I thought. *I'll fucking show you then.*

For the rest of the day, I stayed out, avoided answering your message, and didn't get home until just before midnight. This would make you jumpy, make you wonder why I was staying away, whether my silence had anything to do with your driving that car. You'd come to the conclusion that it did have something to do with it. You'd imagine that I might be so angry that I never wanted to see you again, and that I was ready to kick you out of my home.

As soon as I opened the front door, you came padding over from the living room. Your head was down. I hung up my jacket on the hook without dignifying you with so much as a glance.

'Hi,' you said in a low voice.

'Hi,' I said. 'Do you understand what you're doing? Do you understand how dangerous that was?'

'Yeah, Nick,' you said. 'It was stupid of me.'

'Do you understand what could have happened?'

I turned towards you.

'Yeah, Nick,' you said. 'It was stupid of me.'

I stepped forward and grabbed your chin, lifted your face towards mine. 'Do you understand what I'm saying to you? Promise that you'll never do that again. Never.'

'I promise, Nick,' you said. 'I promise I'll never do it again.'

That's all we said. I went into the bathroom and brushed my teeth. I drew the sliding door to my bedroom, turned off the light and lay down on the bed.

I wasn't angry at you. I wasn't upset. I interlaced my fingers behind my head and gazed out into the darkness.

Half an hour went by.

I got up and went into the hall. Stopped and listened to the sound of your breathing. Then sneaked into the kitchen and poured some cold coffee into a cup. I plugged the computer into the wall socket, sat down at the table, and started writing. I'm the one sitting here with the story. With the experiences. With the fear of what's going to happen to you. Not you. You just want to move on.

I remembered that time, three or four years ago, when you played basketball with that Nazi cop. Remember? We'd invited the police and emergency services to take part in a basketball event at the Malmö Festival. There was quite a crowd around the little court, the sun was shining and the media was there. It was a successful day. Everyone seemed to be enjoying themselves. But it made me uncomfortable that one of the police officers moving among the children had a Nazi background.

In the chaotic early nineties, he used to march with the neo-Nazi demonstrations, which were snagging up Sweden's streets at that time. I was about the same age as you back then; the Nazi cop was ten years older. It was before the Sweden Democrats made parliamentary racism acceptable. At that time, another party, New Democracy, was on the rampage in the tail wind of the financial crisis. Racism found fertile ground in the insecurity into which many Swedes had been cast. People wanted someone to blame, and as usual there were *blattes* available for that.

As for myself, I was relatively well protected, partly because I was difficult to define: whether I was a Swedie, *blatte* or half-blood. Partly also because racism was not quite as distinct where I grew up, the *blattes* and the riffraff lived side by side. But once the team ventured into Skåne's country-side to play our fixtures, we ran head first into contempt. It was not unusual for us to have to escape head over heels in our cramped minibus. I was a skinny boy with a large head, a squeaky voice and a big, dark brown mop of hair. In other words, my prospects of putting up any resistance were non-existent. During our games, the racists sat on the long benches in the claustrophobic and stifling sports halls. Often, their clustered families almost spilled onto the court. Their expletives hailed over us. The atmosphere was frenzied.

They pointed and yelled. We tried to make ourselves look brave, we threw back their insults, but they just laughed at us.

My fantasies about Skåne, this place I liked so much even though I'd hardly been out of the city – a place of open landscapes, patchwork fields, markets, lovely red-painted farmhouses, geese and swallows, spit cake and fried black pudding, oven pancakes with lingonberry jam, and last but not least all the ships heading off to the Continent – these fantasies were more or less killed off in my early teens. Refugee hostels were set alight, a couple of boys were murdered by Nazis, John Ausonius 'the Laser Man' was shooting *blattes* in Stockholm, race and religion were back on the daily menu. And yet, racism at that time was untidy, cloddish, skinheaded, trite, dangerous. Not like today, when it's been blasted into every aspect of our lives, and it over-shadows everything.

It was in this new frightening reality that the Nazi cop appeared in my life. Nothing instilled fear as did the mere sight of this man. Not only because – as far as I knew – he wanted to kill *blattes* like me and was quite open about it. It was also the curious, contradictory fact that he played basketball – the *blatte* sport. How could this add up? It didn't. And that was the unnerving thing.

Sometimes we watched his games; sat in the stands in the sports hall while he ran like an elk down the court. During one game he collided with a Black American guy in the other team, and he had an anger attack: 'You Black bastard!'

his voice reverberated through the sports hall, and there was complete silence. I remember people looking at each other, the sound of scattered nervous laughter. And I remember the referees, at a loss, blowing the whistle for a throw and letting the game go on.

His invective was turned into an inside joke for us boys: *You Black bastard! You brown bastard! You purple bastard!* But it did something to us, his intrusion into our lives.

The Nazi has made a fresh start as a cop. Now I see him on the streets of Malmö.

And I saw him with you that day at the Malmö Festival.

The instinct to protect you was irrational, I knew it. And I controlled myself. That is, until the competitive event kicked off and by coincidence you were paired off with each other. I took you aside and whispered: 'That cop used to be a Nazi. He was going around *Sieg Heiling* when I was your age.'

'Shit,' you said, growing serious. 'For real?'

'Yeah,' I said. 'It's pretty fucked up. That guy was a real skinhead, and now he's a cop.'

You went silent.

'You understand?' I said. 'It's fucked up that an ex-Nazi is a cop, yeah?'

You stared at him, where he was sitting in the stands, smiling, taking a breather among the children. Then you turned to me. 'Yeah, Nick,' you said. 'It's fucked up. But can he play? Straight up? We got a chance?'

That was the only thing you wanted to know. I could have told you the dude had killed five *blatte*s. That he specialized in Black boys, Muslims, like you. It wouldn't have made any difference. The only thing you were interested in, the only thing you could get into your head, the only question in your eyes, was whether he could help you win the competition. Would you and the Nazi cop bring home the glory and the first prize: a box of Ahlgrens chewy cars and an ugly, pink baseball cap?

25

Even though you're only fourteen years old, you have an intimate relationship with death. The number of murdered people that you've been closely involved with number seven or eight. Most of them young.

You're so accustomed to hearing news of shootings and explosions that you react to the violence with a shrug of your shoulders. You regard death as an everyday and almost, it seems, haphazard *occurrence*, which you cannot in any way avoid – nor influence.

But while you'd so far managed to keep the thought of death and its fickleness at arm's length, it proved impossible to be dismissive when it came to the murder of Charles.

Charles had been active in our association and his murder meant that the ultimate evil had now penetrated into your holy sanctum and refuge, meaning your basketball. Because, as you saw it, he was a calm, softly spoken, white middle-aged man who never fucked with anyone, which was how you described him after his death. I was concerned that his murder would shake you to your core.

For this reason, I did everything I could to screen you from it. I was constantly catching myself lying about his death or trivializing it. I heard myself attributing blame to Charles, saying the sort of thing that I hate hearing other people say: 'No one gets shot for no reason, he must have done something.'

I made sure that you weren't reminded of the murder or all the consternation that followed, that you didn't frequent the places where you might bump into Charles's children. I avoided bringing you to the supermarket, where you might be confronted with press hoardings showing photos of his dead body covered with a sheet, or his smiling portrait followed by black letters that pronounced his fate.

I also saw to it that you didn't go to his funeral. You wanted to go so badly. You kept nagging me right up to the last minute. But I said no. I lied: 'The funeral is a private ceremony; only Charles's family and loved ones are allowed to go. You hardly knew him.' This hurt your feelings. Maybe you even wept when I wasn't looking. But the idea of you being there with me in the church among the mourners, the people crying, the coffin and the corpse, was unthinkable.

But it wasn't only for your own protection that I prevented you from being there. I dreaded the thought of having you near me during the ceremony, with your gaze on me, trying to determine what I was feeling.

I'm no good at funerals. Regardless of whether the deceased had his life robbed from him or has died of natural causes, and however close I was to the said person, I feel emotionally empty. I'm even capable of feeling – in most cases, actually – that funerals are cosy, genial occasions. Reality never seems quite as cinematic or the atmosphere as fraught and loaded with meaning as when someone has died. All the factors come into play, especially during a Christian burial: the internal capaciousness of the chapel, the lit candles, the acoustics accentuating every slight sound – the organ music, the preaching of the pastor, the sobbing, heels against flagstones. On no other occasion am I ever so dressed up, so like an actor. I wear my black overcoat with the collar folded up, a black suit, tie, highly polished black shoes and a white shirt. My enthusiasm starts picking up even before I set off for church, as I sort through my clothes in the wardrobe. I fantasize about moving among the mourners that come towards me, embracing me, seeking my consolation. The climax comes when I walk down the aisle and place the rose on the coffin lid. I'm at the centre of things. Everyone is looking at me. Struck by the dignity of my movements, how strong I must be because I do not weep over the dead. The reason why I am relishing all this is that I'm measuring myself against the other members of the congregation, who are more devastated than me, even though we're mourning the same loss. They're weaker than me. They sink into despair, while I'm held up by inner strength. This realization is grand.

After the funeral, I hurried across the courtyard outside the church; slipped around the corner where I'd left my bicycle, unlocked it and pedalled off.

The wind and the high speed at which I was travelling made my coat flap like a mantle. The cold, the drizzle of rain, quickly penetrated my thin garments, and by the time I turned into the parking area with the sports centre sprawling on the other side, I was frozen stiff.

To compensate for the unfairness of you not being able to attend, I'd booked a training session for a couple of hours after the funeral. I was planning to behave the same as ever, suitably jovial, calm and focused on the task at hand.

The idea was that we'd get changed, talk about which restaurant we were going to afterwards, and then I thought I'd suggest rounding off the evening by going to the movies.

And yet it also struck me that my plan wasn't thought through and might even be idiotic. I couldn't just act indifferent. I'd just been to a friend's funeral. A friend who'd been murdered. The only reasonable thing would be to seem downhearted. Anyway, I thought: wasn't it totally suspect to pick a day like this for some damn practice? Why hadn't we just stayed at home? What was I trying to hide here?

As I cycled down the gravelled pedestrian path and you came into view, I arranged a gloomy face. You stood outside the entrance, with your arms wrapped around your body to keep warm. You were wearing spring clothes: a flimsy jacket with the hood drawn up and laced around your face. Grey velour trousers, a green glove on your right hand and trainers. Your face lit up and you took a step towards me, but when I didn't respond, you looked down. I leaned the bicycle against the building, climbed the first set of stairs onto the flat mid-section and gave you a hug. I unlocked the door and we walked through the darkness of the sports hall without uttering a word. You were nervous, I could hear it in your steps. You wanted to establish some contact with me, but you couldn't think of anything to say. So we went into the changing room, and then the silence grew too difficult to bear.

'Are you sad, Nick?' you probed. 'Are you sad about Charles being dead?'

I looked at you. 'No, brother,' I said. 'I'm good.'

That wasn't the answer you were expecting. You dwelled on it for a bit. Then you asked: 'Will you care if I die?'

I flinched. Then I walked up to you, hugged you. 'What are you saying?' I said. 'Of course I'll care. You're my kid, Elijah. Never think that way again.'

You laughed. 'I know, Nick,' you said.

You turned your back on me and reached into your bag, pulled out your vest and shorts and put the ball on the bench next to you. I stood behind you. Looked at your scrawny body. Your thin arms, shoulders. Your skinny legs. That shaggy Mohican hairstyle.

I said: 'I just have to take a leak, bro. Start warming up, I'll be out in a minute.'

I opened the toilet door, closed and locked it, turned on the water at full pressure. I heard the ball bouncing against the parquet. Heard the rattling sound as it struck the hoop. I turned towards the mirror and looked into my eyes. Then I squatted to the floor, pressed my hands into my face, and broke down in tears.

26

One night at half past eight you came charging through the front door, crying. I hugged you and asked you what had happened. We went into the living room to talk.

Between sobs, you told me that the police had threatened you. Abbe, Josef and you had been walking in the city and you were just about to part ways when a policeman turned up.

'He was really cocky, Nick,' you said. 'He laughed at us, and he told us to stay right there. There were some other police further up ahead; they were looking. We didn't get why they stopped us and Abbe got cocky back at them: "You can't just hold us like this," he said. "You don't have the right." The police just laughed at us and said, "We can do whatever we like." He said he could take us back to the police station or to Bok Forest and there wasn't a thing we could do about it. That's what he said, Nick. It was really creepy. 'Cos he was calm when he said it. He was just, like, smiling the whole time.'

'Is that why you're upset?' I said, still unsure whether you were telling me the whole truth. 'The police often mess with you, don't they?'

'It's not the police I'm afraid of, Nick,' you said. 'Or, not really afraid of them, anyway. They stop us sometimes; they say mean shit, like our mums are whores, we're *blattes*, and all that. They do, Nick. They call you a *blatte* and they say you should fuck your mother. They say that stuff 'cos they know people hate it when someone says something about their mother. It's like they want us to flip out. But I don't flip out; I know the way they work. But it eats me. It hurts more and more. Not the first time. Not the second. But the tenth. It really hurts that time, Nick. I don't get why they hate me.'

We talked for over an hour. And soon it emerged, as I'd suspected, that your emotional reaction was also based on something else.

It seems that you can put up with a couple of setbacks in the day. You can end up in a fight, you can be demeaned, exposed to a few wrongs, without having your resistance broken down. Then, after that, you need to recover yourself the way a boxer does between the rounds before the fight resumes. Few things frighten you more than confrontation with the police. Although it's not really a case of confrontation. The amassment of violence is one-sided. And this feeling – the impotence of not being able to defend yourself, strike back or do a runner – makes the encounters particularly unpleasant. In this respect the fear you have for the police is quite different from what you feel towards those who hand out punishment on the street, in the playground, and in the adult world. If you enter into conflict with young people from the area who have a tendency to utilize heavier violence than you ever would, you have the choice either to fight or take flight. The same thing applies to grown-ups who humiliate you.

Your relationship to the world of adults is laced with conflict. Or rather, you lack respect for adults. You're afraid of them. You have few reasons to believe that they want your best. And so you're quite right to be suspicious and question their intentions and regard every adult as a potential force for ill.

That you can't win the fight against the adult world does not prevent you from trying. Many times you've ended up in conflict, both of a verbal and a physical kind. Any such behaviour is impossible in relation to the police. And that was the reason why your meeting with the threatening policeman was especially frightening. You didn't have a chance. And still, that was not what brought you to your knees. What caused it was the sum of all the accumulated assaults of the day.

It had started at school. In the national media your school is ranked as one of the worst in Sweden. It's a fact, while also a stigmatizing classification. Turning it into click-bait journalism is loathsome.

Your school is a shameful blot on the whole country. Just to put one's foot in those narrow corridors with the nailed-up or barred windows, to see the barbed wire on the roofs and the walls and the gates that enclose the main school building, to pick up the stench of the dank toilets and bodies moving through the cramped and badly ventilated corridors, constantly watched by the fish-eye surveillance cameras, is a claustrophobic experience. The children are like convicts.

When the national inspectorate went to the school a year or so ago, they criticized the management and relevant local politicians in so many instances that one might even come to the conclusion that the collapse had been intentional. Criticisms included: a poor working and studying environment, a lack of commitment by the teachers and fear of the children (there were repeated references to teachers being beaten or teachers withdrawing to their offices and not daring to intervene when conflicts arose), threats, violence, the general feeling of insecurity, poor academic results (fewer than half of middle-school students went on to upper school), the teachers' low expectations of their students (resulting in the students' low expectations of themselves), the physical decay of the buildings and the prison-like feel of the place.

Last year some thirty fires were started at the school. It's not a statistic that particularly stands out. Setting things alight has become a fad at many of Malmö's worst-performing schools in the poorer parts of the city. Kids set fire to curtains or bins in the toilets, fire and smoke spread, fire alarms are triggered, classes are interrupted and the schools are evacuated.

The difference between your school and many of the others is that your school is in an especially poor state. It's more or less unchanged since the sixties, and fire safety can't be guaranteed. If a fire broke out and you found yourself in one of the rooms without an emergency exit and bars in front of the windows, or if panic broke out and there was a stampede in the narrow corridors, you'd risk being trampled or burned alive.

Not long ago you complained of the smoke preventing you from focusing on your studies. I remember how you put it: 'The smell of the smoke stings my brain. I can't think about maths if I have to think about a fire.' I realized that the situation was serious, and I thought about contacting the media. But it was a double-edged sword. If the problem was taken seriously, the pyromaniacs would be caught and stringently punished – with all the usual lack of responsibility that one sees in the Swedish school system: first the school management would report the kids to the police, expel them, apologize for any mistakes that were made, then emphasize that they'd review the fire safety regulations now that the little devils had been taken out of the picture. But as you were highly likely to be one of the those setting the fires, this would put you in trouble. Better to go on setting fire to things, I reasoned slightly dubiously, than to end up in their registry.

One night, when we sat in my kitchen practising vocabulary, you said:

'You know what, Nick, last year my school was ranked the second worst in Sweden. Now the school that used to be number one has been closed down. So we're in first place.'

I said: 'You mean the last place?'

You said: 'No. We're the best at being the worst.'

That sentence etched itself into me. The best at being the worst. You put your finger on what happens to many of the children that are pushed by society into the far reaches of existence. It's impossible to go along passively with the surrounding world's view of one as a worthless human being. Nor is it very easy to shake off a stigma like that once it's burned itself into one's psyche.

The worst school in Sweden says something about the pupils that go there. It says, these are the worst children in Sweden.

You relate to the branding in just the same way as all people do. On the one hand you need to consider your 'worstness', turning it into a badge of honour, something desirable that you can boast about. But at the same time, you embody this deeply demoralizing picture, you confirm the prejudices and live up to the expectations.

There's also a third way of handling the dilemma – that of proving the haters wrong by deciding to exceed them, becoming a model pupil and behaving impeccably. Acquiring the tools to escape the area and reinventing oneself. But such thoughts are best kept to oneself. The slightest attempt to put them into action is dangerous. At the risk of being slightly crude in one's categorization, the majority of the children at your school can be divided into two social groups: the quiet ones with poor self-confidence and low self-esteem and the loud ones with poor self-confidence and low self-esteem. Tooth and nail, you've fought your way into the latter category. At the expense of other children's security, by fright-ening, hitting and humiliating them, you've positioned yourself at the top of the hierarchy. You're terrified of the implications of any demotion. You know there's no way of placing yourself outside of the existing order without punishment.

If you were to suddenly sit at the front of the classroom, take your studies seriously and talk respectfully to adults, you'd not only be walking out of a social context where you are welcome, but it would also be turned against you. Yours would be an unforgivable deceit, a crime that would be punished immediately and brutally. As soon as your associates, the ones that call you *brother*, noticed that you were moving away, a number of them would team up against you, freeze you out, and do harm to you and your reputation.

If you're brave and resistant and you have the capacity to withstand the blows and humiliations because of your decision that there's happiness beyond the misery and that you're worthy of finding it, you'll soon face an even mightier enemy: your own self. After all, you also believe that you're worthless, unloved and the worst of Sweden. The risk you take if you try to overturn these conceptions of yourself is that you fail to do it, and then they prove to be quite right. You can't subject yourself to all that pain. You daren't. It's better to fuck up the whole thing. Avoid heaven because of your fear of hell.

The thing that made it all too much for you today was not the degrading state of your school in its own right, but something said by one of those who make the rules there. During the lunch break you'd had a dispute with a teacher. It was a trivial thing, you explained. 'I just wanted to joke around with her.' But rather than shouting, weeping or threatening you with expulsion, which you were expecting, she turned ice cold. She looked you up and down and then, before turning around and walking off, she said: 'What a disgusting human being you are.'

You had different reactions when the policeman stopped you. Abbe had flared up, you told me. He swore that he'd take revenge. Said you'd smash the windows at the police station or blow up the whole bloody thing with a bomb. Josef had been quieter; he was shaken, you said. 'He didn't say anything, not while the police were carrying on and not afterwards either. He's pretty sensitive, Nick, he takes that shit in and it stays inside him.'

Afterwards you left and went to the sports hall to train.

As you took that short walk from Gustav Adolfs Plaza through the churchyard past the City Library and across the big road, you must have been fighting to keep your emotions in check. You must have been trying to convert those para-lysing feelings of anxiety and despair into something useful, such as aggression and hatred. You'd been humiliated, your peace of mind had been disturbed. It doesn't take much to make your cup overflow.

As you went into the front entrance of the sports centre and saw that the women's team were at practice it must have made you feel nervous.

Their trainer has a particular problem with *blatte* boys in the sports hall. You've experienced this first-hand on countless occasions. The club allows people to hang out in the halls while other teams are training, on the condition that they don't cause any disturbance and that the baskets are given up whenever they're needed. But there are often tensions and arguments. Coaching staff who haven't been around the block enough times start roaring as soon as some outsider bounces a ball a few times too many. It must be some Swedie thing, I often think. It's this thing of going to pieces with terror because you think something might be taken away from you.

You left your bag on the long bench and started shooting at one of the hoops. It only took twenty minutes before the trainers and the team captain were all over you. Three grown-ups screaming right into your face.

'It was like I'd murdered their families or something,' you said. 'They kept yelling until their faces were bright red.'

I could see them before my very eyes. I remembered all the times grown-ups had lost their cool about some shitty little thing and ended up yelling at me in that exact same way. I could see them standing over me, their eyes about to pop out of their skulls. They screamed at you that you had no respect, that you could never again come to the sports hall during their training sessions.

'It was really fucking embarrassing,' you said. 'Especially because everyone else in the sports hall was standing there watching.'

I asked what you'd done. You didn't stop playing the second time they told you, you admitted.

'I should have, Nick, I wasn't quick enough. But they were

such fucking hobos, right. They just wanted to give me grief, put me down. First time they told me I didn't grab the ball quick enough, and that was my fault. But the second time I didn't even know they'd stopped the game, I didn't hear, I was totally into my own thing. Then I saw them running towards me. Then they got in my face, screaming like idiots. It was too much, bro, honestly. They just hung their shitty little lives on me.'

After this dressing-down they kicked you out. You took your belongings, went into the coat room and got changed. You said you wanted to smash all the windows; you thought about picking up the shoe shelf and chucking it out through the glass. You felt so humiliated and fucking angry, you said. Wanted to create complete chaos for everyone in the sports hall.

Maybe you were already crying then. Maybe you clenched your jaw and thought you wouldn't give anyone the satisfaction of seeing you bawl. That's the only important thing, you thought. *Bite your lip, Elijah. Don't give them the satisfaction of seeing you cry. Soon you'll be back home with Nick.*

27

Since you came home crying I have been taken over by two overwhelming feelings.

One of them is tenderness for you. A deepening love, maybe, because the insight into the contempt you have to put up with, which surrounds you, has penetrated more deeply into me. The other feeling is shame.

The first thing I did the following morning, to get us both into a better mood, was to deal with your bed situation. The gloomy atmosphere, which had lingered in the flat, would be eased if once and for all I solved the dilemma of how you were sleeping. I called around among some friends to ask if anyone had a camp bed they could do without. I scored a hit, and when you came home the bed was made up and ready in the living room. On the other hand the mattress that had come with the bed was so flimsy that you sank into the springs when you lay on it. I said that I had a thicker mattress in the attic, which might possibly be a bit disgusting, but would probably be okay to use instead. You wanted this, so we went up to the attic and carried it downstairs. I rolled it out on the floor, had a good look at it, told you that it had once been full of bed bugs, and you had to be attentive if you started itching. I covered it with a clean sheet and put the duvet and pillow on top.

I've rarely seen you so happy. You were quite radiant all evening. You threw yourself on the bed. Stood up. Threw yourself on it all over again.

Against the shame, on the other hand, there's no antidote. The fears and mechanisms that make it possible for me to behave badly towards you are the same fears and mechanisms that make society behave badly towards you. I search for those traits of yours that make it easier for me to push you away, minimize your value, and render you harmless.

It pains me to think about it.

Pains me, because just like you and the boys you socialize with, I want to identify myself as someone who distances himself from society and its evils; I want to be a part of the resistance, and the good. To find that I'm involved in the same power games and domineering behaviour, and that when the chips are down and I feel threatened I only want to hold on to what I perceive as mine, and protect myself – it's a difficult thing to take in.

It made no difference that I had done some good things for you, that I backed you emotionally and financially, or that, as you'd often said, I was your best friend. My mastery techniques, my consummate micro-aggressions and need to control things, could not be denied.

These last few days I've been feeling that I can't manage to be both good and strong. I've convinced myself that I'm too weak, too much of a milksop, fundamentally so damaged by the warring circumstances in my life that I've never been allowed to be as good as I really am.

As you grow older and you listen to the self-appointed community leaders in Sweden's *blatte* ghettoes, you'll hear them declaim about how great it is to live there, what a stonking good community feeling we have, how cool it is in the ghetto, what fine people we really are, this being a tame attempt to maintain some honour among people who are increasingly demonized and deprived of the ability to live dignified lives. You'll hear a terrible, counterproductive romanticization, a fine polish of the most neglected places in Sweden. There is a possible argument that injustice can make one humble, help one gain insights and experiences, and broaden the general understanding of what it means to be a human being. And, certainly, there's a revolutionary explosiveness in the underdog perspective. But all this can just as well force you to sign off on your humanity, your possibilities of living as a good person, and instead, at worst, you'll become a cold-hearted monster. By this worst-case scenario, you'll end up killing other children because your heart has been hardened and your view of human life blunted to such an extent that you can snuff out a life without self-recrimination.

Vilhelm Moberg writes:

No one should try to make poverty a thing of beauty to my eyes. Poverty is merely ugly and humiliating and embittering to a human being; the legend of its fair appearance and good moral workings have been created by the rich.

My conclusion is, that I'm insufficient but also courageous because in taking care of you I am exceeding my own nature.

It sounds heroic.

It *is* heroic.

I am taking you on because I don't want you to die. Because I care about you – that is, love you – and I'm aware of the fact that you may die, or wipe yourself out by extinguishing another person. I've taken you on because society has created this world of walls, walls which close in on you, and I imagine myself leaning forward, reaching down with my hand and, risking a fall myself into the abyss, hoisting you up to safety. It's not an entirely inaccurate picture. But it would be just as true to elicit an image of myself as a child down there at the bottom, with the walls of the class system slowly closing around me, and how as a grown-up I am now coming to my own aid. It's a cliché and it's trivial: in you I see myself. I am taking you on and consoling you as a way of taking on and comforting myself.

When you came home the other day and you were crying in the hall because society can't see any value in a *blatte* kid like you, I felt a pinprick of happiness. Yeah, that's exactly what I felt. Happiness. I did feel sorry for you, but I was also pleased. Your misery gave me the chance to comfort you, while at the same time giving myself some comfort too.

It was the most wonderful feeling.

28

My nurturing of you, Elijah, is political. An act of resistance. A 'fuck you' to Sweden.

It feels incredible to look at it that way. I'm *doing* politics. I'm not peddling opinions. Not taking part in demonstrations. I don't belong to a political party. No. I'm someone who takes practical action, someone who allows a stranger's child to come and live in my home. I'll do without some of the comforts for the sake of something bigger than myself. That's politics. Politics with the human body as the starting point. Politics as the antithesis of hunger and humiliation.

The body comes first, and then morality. The body is the starting point for morality. Or, as someone has written on the graffiti wall by the junkie roundabout in Möllan, *First food, then morals.*

It's Brecht: *First food, then ethics.*

It's Vreeswijk: *Streamers and placards can't be eaten.*

It's Bob Marley: *A hungry mob is an angry mob.*

It's Orwell: *An empty belly leaves no room for spiritual speculation.*

Hunger. Not like some neo-liberal metaphor for will and drive, the passionate belief in the ability of the individual to be compelled by a sufficient level of *hunger* to extract them-self from all sorts of predicaments. Rather just hunger as in the absence of food, the need to eat, starvation.

A few years ago I read *German Autumn* by Stig Dagerman:

> One asked Germans living in cellars if things were better under Hitler, and these Germans answered: yes. One asked a drowning man if he was better off when he was standing on the quay, and he answered: yes. If you ask someone starving on two slices of bread per day if he was better off when he was starving on five, you will doubtless get the same answer.

Can the hungry be held responsible for actions they've taken on an empty stomach? Can one really expect people, who don't know where their next meal is coming from, to be incorrigible?

This is politics. Everything else is bullshit. Everything, all *political thinking* that does not base itself on the fundamental needs of humanity, lacks legitimacy. Is corrupt.

These arguments suit me very well. I'm not the sort of person who just talks and whines. I push my fingers into the loam. I work in silence. I step in where society fails, snatching *blattes* from the jaws of whiteness and getting them fed at Chicken Cottage.

It's politics!

And it's fantastic to think that I'm one of those political human beings. So fantastic that, earlier today, when we met at Barista after your game to drink some hot chocolate, I wanted to share my exuberant happiness.

You'd be uninterested in what I had to say, I knew that in advance. But I had to get it all out. I was bursting with new insights, I had to listen to myself speaking them out loud. As soon as we sat down, needing no prompt, I started talking. At first I maintained a conversational tone, but then, as one nugget of wisdom after another burst forth, I grew increasingly loud and fired up. At first you were drawn in, you listened with concentration and tried to follow my main line of reasoning. But you lost your focus before too long. I didn't give a damn. I went on talking. For fifteen minutes I carried on at full blast, skidding from one subject to another. Then, you interrupted me.

'Nick,' you said, 'are you good with me borrowing your phone and checking YouTube for a bit? My head's, like, pretty tired.'

'Yeah, yeah,' I said. 'That's no problem, you do your thing. But my battery's quite low. Are you good with reading something instead? I've got some books with me. You can pick whichever one you want.' I opened my bag and put a pile on the table. 'This book is about Sweden in the sixties,' I said, 'the so-called 68 Movement. It's quite interesting. And this one might seem a bit hippyish because it's about . . . or I mean . . . there's no real plot in it. You get to stay in a woman's head for a few days, her tangle of thoughts. Also fairly interesting.'

You looked at me. Dead eyes.

'Okay,' you said. 'I'll take this one, then.'

You picked up Malcolm X's autobiography, which I'd been using in my teaching that day. You rose from the chair and went over to the bench, where you stretched out and started reading.

For a while I watched you. I didn't say a word, wasn't thinking of anything in particular.

The staff were whizzing by with their jingling trays of glasses, cups and saucers. They glared at you when they almost stumbled over the ball that you'd left on the floor.

It struck me that I'd never seen you read a book before. Never in all our years together had you held an open book in your hands. Sometimes you let your eyes sweep across the bindings on my shelf, but you never picked one out and started to read. One evening about a week ago you opened *Black Skin, White Masks* by Frantz Fanon. Quickly, almost as if horrified, you closed it very hard. Books, reading, writing, intellectual curiosity, politics, economics, history, mathematics – all the things that remind you of how stupid and uneducated you are, the worst kid in Sweden – are rejected by you.

You're aware that you ought to have more insight into the processes that are dictating your life. To see through the reasons why your school is the worst in Sweden, why the police are hounding you, why Swedies avoid you like the plague and why other *blattes* are always staring you out, and why sometimes feel so awful. The information is out there. You know that. At the same time it's out of reach for you. You can seek it out, find it. But when you find it, it's as if it slips out of your hands once more.

*   *   *

I thought about this while you were lying on that bench in the cafe, reading. It was a lovely little moment, but also disheartening.

You're the loneliest person I know, Elijah.

I never thought that way about you before. But I think it's right.

You're the loneliest person I know.

If I were to ask you to reel off all the people who are indispensable to you, people you can count on and trust, people you love, you wouldn't have to use very many fingers.

The same must also apply the other way. If you counted the people to whom you are indispensable, who know you deep down, love you, and have enough insight into your life to know how you are feeling, they wouldn't be many.

You're not only the loneliest person I know, Elijah. You are also the most unloved.

It's dangerous to write this. I feel that in my body. And I can't possibly know if it's true.

I think it's true.

And I can take that even further.

Not only are you alone and comparatively unloved, you also have a directly repelling effect on the people you meet. In some circles you're appreciated. Especially among some of the kids in your area, a couple of players on your team. Yet on the whole you're not a particularly well-liked person. The children look up to you but this is counterbalanced by an equal amount of fear. You do have friends who'd back you up if you got into trouble, but they're easily counted. A couple of adults would be there for you too: a few trainers, some of my friends and colleagues who've known you for a long time. But none of them unconditionally. They can't get close to you, they're unaware of your circumstances, your relationships are superficial.

One could ask oneself, how many people would be devastated if you died?

Obviously I'm not in a position to know the exact number.

Your family would be devastated. Especially your mother. For others in your orbit it would be a terrible feeling, to have a young person that they know cease to exist. But apart from the sense of shock, few people's lives would change because you weren't there.

And isn't this a measure of how strong our relationships are to others: whose lives would be shattered by our death?

Whose lives would be shattered by your death, Elijah?

What do the above insinuations have to do with you and me?

They are the actual prerequisite for my taking you into my care.

Few people are concerned enough about you to pry into our arrangements. No one knows how badly I've treated you from time to time. No one knows that you've been sleeping on my sofa for months. No one judges, no one praises. No one knows how terrible you sometimes feel.

This is also a gauge of the love we have in our lives: the number of people who know we're suffering when we're suffering. And the number of people who are concerned about it, who'll do everything in their power to make the suffering stop.

One can toy with the idea of what would happen if you drifted about on Malmö's streets through the nights. If you slept in stairwells, parks, bus stops, refuse rooms.

If one day you decided everything had to come to an end. During the summer holiday when routines and schedules tend to fall by the wayside, if you decided to head down to the sea in order to drown yourself, it's not so unlikely that it would take weeks or even months before anyone would seriously start enquiring about your whereabouts.

29

You talk less and less with your mother. Whenever contact is made, it's usually your initiative. It's mostly about practicalities, your need to pick something up in the flat or ask her for money. When you call her, when you lift the phone to your ear, you're dreading it. And when she answers, you overwhelm her with accusations. It's unpleasant to have to listen to it. The conversations never last very long. The tone is never conciliatory. Afterwards, you're upset.

'She makes me so fucking angry, Nick,' you say. 'She just talks shit. I'm so tired of her.'

You're burning with frustration and anger. We talk for a while. And once the anger has dispersed and you lower your defences, you can make space for grief. You say you love her. You love her so much that it hurts. You say you're worried that she's going to come to harm, that she'll die. Your voice falters.

'I love her so fucking much, Nick,' you say. 'You don't get how much I love her. Mum's always been there for me. But now when it's my turn to be there for her, I can't do it, she doesn't want me to.'

'No,' I say, 'but it doesn't have anything to do with you. And it's not about wanting something. Your mum can't imagine anything better than just being happy with you. You have to accept that your mother's sick; only she can take responsibility for getting better. What's needed here is that she recognizes the problem and gets on with it. The best thing you can do is think about yourself, establish some clear boundaries, and be honest about your emotions, honest about how you're feeling. That's all you can do. She has to solve the rest of it.'

That's how it goes when we talk. And always, without any exceptions, these conversations finish with you asking me, do I think your mother's going to die? And then I lie. I say that the chances of her getting better are much improved now that she doesn't have to take responsibility for you, and she can focus on herself. I say that she'll soon realize what she runs the risk of losing here, and that this may spur her on to stop. I don't share what I'm really thinking. What I truly believe. Namely, that things will probably never be entirely resolved. Your absence, your withdrawal, the fact that you left her, is highly likely to intensify the anguish and guilt she must be feeling. But there's also a risk of it generating feelings of guilt in you. For even though you're a child, a young person seeking security, and even though your withdrawal from your mother is justified, you've nonetheless left her, abandoned her.

And you'll have to live with that for the rest of your life.

30

Every year, the organization that I work for is awarded a minor sum of money from the local council to be used for 'the encouragement of social integration among young people'. In return for these crumbs that we're given, we undertake to come once per year to a meeting of the council, where we describe what we've been doing with the taxpayers' money. Today was one such day.

Thirty people, mostly local politicians but also ordinary citizens, were present. The room reminded me of a classroom, although it was more cramped. The atmosphere was as dense as a sauna, and as chilly as a cellar.

When my name appeared on the agenda, the chair called me to the podium. I got out my computer from my bag, then hooked up the beamer, which came to life with a loud buzzing sound. On the projection screen adjacently behind me, there appeared an image of seven children. They were laughing hysterically, holding out their cones like trophies, ice cream smeared all around their mouths. I'd picked that photograph because it's impossible to look at it without filling up with a warm feeling. I thought it would make the participants relax and smile a bit.

Far from it.

I introduced myself. Told them about the organization and what we do. Showed them the next slide, a picture of three smiling Black girls, each with a hoop in their hand. I said that no other organization in Malmö worked with as many girls from disadvantaged parts of the city. I boasted. Reeled off statistics. The next slide was of four pensioners holding carrier bags of food. They were old Kockums workers, old-school grafters, lovely old blokes with missing teeth. 'One million kronor,' I said. 'That's what we put into schemes to help elderly people every year. In other words, we don't only support children and young people, we help all people who've fallen on hard times.'

A hand shot up into the air. A Conservative hand.

I continued. I said that we activate about four thousand people per year. If one included our events, the number would be much greater. Hundreds of thousands, according to Malmö City Hall.

'Yes,' I said, pointing at the Conservative.

'I think I speak for us all when I say, you seem to be running a good project here.' He nodded, first at his party colleagues on the long-table next to him, and then towards the rest of the room. On the left, at the other long table, sat five Social Democrats in a row. Behind them sat two Liberals. And in the middle of the room, in front of me at a lone table, sat a Sweden Democrat. I had seen the other politicians before, some of them on so many occasions and for such a length of time that their faces had coagulated on my retina and become synonymous with Malmö's political life. But not the Sweden Democrat. He was about the same age as me. Thinning hair, bloated and pale as a drowned man. During the entire presentation he'd sat with his face towards the window, his arms crossed. Now he looked directly at me. But not in a hostile way. He looked sympathetic.

The reason for my not having seen the man before was obviously that the Sweden Democrats in Malmö had been growing, claiming more and more seats on local committees.

'I have two questions,' said the Conservative. 'What exactly do you mean by "fallen on hard times"? And then I want to know why there are only brown children in the photographs?'

A Social Democrat snorted, in a rough-hewn Skåne accent: 'Oh, what are you on about?'

'What?' the Conservative snorted back in a just-as-heavy Skåne accent. 'You know what I'm saying.'

Afterwards, at the Café Hollandia, I stuffed down two creamy soft buns in two seconds flat. You called on FaceTime.

'Nick!' you belly-laughed as soon as the camera had turned itself on.

'What?' I said. At the same time I caught sight of my face in the box, to the right of the screen. I had cream on my nose and across half of my moustache.

'Look at this!' you said, turning the camera towards the kitchen.

It was clinically clean.

Not only had you put away bags of bread, cereal cartons, the cloth bag of sunflower seeds into the larder and emptied the dishwasher, you had also wiped down the counter and scrubbed the in-grown dirt off the hob, leaving it gleaming white. And the floor was still damp from where the mop had passed over.

'Oh my God!' I burst out. 'Shit, that looks really nice!'

'Right?! I've been going for it all afternoon.'

'You're growing in my eyes, Elijah. Every day that goes by I'm feeling more and more proud of you. You know that?'

31

Abbe has been picked for the county team. This means he'll be going on tour in a month, with a chance of being accepted into the national youth team. He was so happy that he didn't open his gob for half an hour after getting the notification, which was a personal record for him.

We took the bus to Rosengård. I bought some cheap underwear and a pack of socks for you in the shopping centre, then we sat down on a bench on the plaza, with pizzas on our laps.

You giggled about the people who were passing by, commenting in whispers about their appearance. A limping old man with a potato nose, pulling a shopping trolley. A stooped woman wearing a veil. A boy with a bin bag filled with deposit cans thrown over his shoulder – you elaborated an entire life story for him ('I'll let him clean my pool').

I thought about other kids your age who like to point out what cars are 'theirs'. Cars they have fantasies of owning one day: 'That BMW is mine!' or 'That's the kinda Merc I'm gonna have!' But you aren't like that. Instead, you tend to comment on aspects of people that you consider to be especially ugly or discrepant.

Next, you started discussing who were the most despised *blattes* in Sweden. Whether this would be Arabs, in other words Muslims, or Africans – or, God forbid, a combination of the two. Oh yes, you affirmed, all the while laughing, to be Black and a Muslim in Sweden was the very worst thing you could be. You rated passers-by. Blond and white was right at the top of the scale: ten points (loved). Black and Muslim: zero points (hated).

'She's an easy nine, that one.'

'That lump of coal over there is a minus one.'

'That one by the car . . . I'm being nice, I'll give him a three.'

You graded yourselves. Abbe, who's an Arab, got a two. Josef, who's half-Arab and half-Thai, got three and a half. But you were the most hated, you all decided.

'I'm light-skinned, brother,' you tried.

'No, no,' Abbe countered. 'You look like an African and an Arab. And you're a Muslim. You're the most hated, brother. You're a minus fifty!'

The clouds towered up and the wind was whining between the houses. During the bus journey home you didn't say a lot. You sat with your forehead against the window, your eyes darting between objects swishing by outside.

The life expectancy of the people living in the place where we boarded the bus, and those where we got off, diverged by eight years. What this means, I calculated, is that the years increase at the blistering pace of one year per bus stop between Rosengård and us.

I hate things being this way.

The skies opened when we arrived. First, it was a curtain of vertically falling, chilled rain. Then a sudden hailstorm, whose grains of ice were as large as marbles and chased us all the way home.

Once you'd fallen asleep I stood there in the doorway, looking at you. You were in a foetal position. Your untidy hair stuck up from under the duvet, which was pulled slightly over your face. You were breathing heavily.

32

When you become an adult, Elijah, I want you to remember one thing. All the people around you were aware of your situation. They all knew that you were living in conditions that were too difficult for a child. And that they could have cost you your life.

They all knew. Every one of them. But no one did what was required to make things better for you. I want you to think about this when you're older and you look back at your childhood, if you survive it. They all knew. They all let you down.

Ever since you portioned out your own levels of odiousness on that bench, I've been thinking about what you said. And you were right. Sweden hates you, Elijah.

All the ponderous questions. How it's possible that you should be able to live as you do, knowing what it might lead to. That a young person's dreams and body can be shredded without any general concern, or a requirement to make sure that it's stopped from ever happening again, can only be explained with those words: Sweden hates you.

There's no other explanation.

It makes me furious and it sends me into despair. I want

to explain this to you. I want to storm into the living room and yell: 'Sweden hates you, Elijah! That's why sometimes you feel so fucking awful!'

You'd probably just laugh if I said it like that, because it sounds so ludicrous, and because you'd think I was only saying it to mess with you. Or you'd be offended, shocked and startled – *Why are you saying something so horrible, Nick?* You'd have a hard time understanding what I was trying to convey to you.

In *The Souls of Black Folk*, the writer and sociologist W. E. B. Du Bois asks the rhetorical question, which, he feels, hangs in the air and penetrates into the psyche of Black people: how does it feel to be a problem? Du Bois writes that Black people develop a dual consciousness. On the one hand there's an inner, subjective understanding of who they are. And on the other hand, an external, objective, reductive idea.

A conversation about how Sweden hates you, and how you can manage to live with this insight, might be introduced with precisely this question.

But in your case, it's not about your being the *problem* in an indistinct form, but very much the *problem* in its essence – everything is blamed on you. The hollowing out of the welfare system, the failure of schools, unemployment, the waiting lines for healthcare, an oversubscribed national health service, pensions.

It's quite easy to imagine walking up to you, and just blurting out the question: 'How does it feel to be the problem?'

You'd stare at me in wonder.

'What do you mean, Nick?' you'd say. 'I don't get what you mean. Whose problem am I? What have I done? What's happened?'

'Nothing's happened,' I'd tell you. 'Or, I mean, something is happening, it happens all the time. And that's what I want to talk to you about. I want to talk to you about how racism works, the way it's been smoked into every cell in your body, and how class determines your every movement, how you're at the very bottom of the hierarchy. And your reasoning when you were sitting on that bench was correct: Sweden does hate you. Do you remember what you said when you came home that time, and told me that the police had been harassing you? You remember? You said: "I don't understand why they hate me." Do you remember saying that? I know the answer to that question.'

But even that approach would be difficult. Serious and cryptic. Better if I rely on humour, one *blatte* to another. And talk to you the way you were talking to each other on that bench.

'You're a *blatte*, brother,' I could say. 'And that's what I want to talk to you about. I understand it's not like news to you, your being a *blatte*. But what I want to say is, you're not just any old *blatte*, you're the very worst kind of *blatte*.'

You'd have a giggle about that. When I called you a *blatte* your face would light up with a smile, and you'd try hard to come up with a clever retort.

'Ha-ha, Nick, and that's coming from you! You're a *blatte* as well!'

'Admittedly so,' I'd say, 'but I want to talk to you about

what you, Abbe and Josef realized yourselves. The deeper significance of what you said. That there are levels, grades. *Blattes* are treated differently in Sweden. Some *blattes* are worth less than others and you rank lowest. I know you were only joking about it. But it was correct. And I think it's important that you absorb the insight, build your life and your relationship to the world on the basis of the odiousness in which you're held. And understand the layers, how there are other factors that also come into play. You belong to the underclass. You live in a *blatte* area, you hang out with other *blattes*, you talk and behave like a *blatte*, and you come from Sweden's most loathed city of *blattes*, Malmö. You're hyperactive and you have a violent streak. You don't have one thing in your favour, man. I want you to think about what that means and what consequences it could have.'

Or else I'm just best advised to get down to brass tacks with you. Forget about all the thought-out rhetorical inventiveness, the gallows humour we so often use when talking about difficult things. That *blatte* lingo, which I'm so tired of.

'You feel bad, Elijah. You have a feeling that the world is against you, that people hate you, because this is precisely how it is. Maybe it sounds a bit drastic. But, actually, there's no other person who so completely represents our fears in Sweden as a young brown, or Black, Muslim. And he's you. Yes – you're the actual mental image of the worst possible human being. You look like – and you make people think of – the gang member, the robber, the rapist, the cold-blooded murderer.'

* * *

147

At the same time there's an even more frightening thought, which scuppers this whole line of reasoning. Sweden does not care enough about you to hate you. The paradox is: you'd be even more hated if you died than if you lived.

Your murder, Elijah, would lead to a situation where suspicions were cast on you, and preconceptions about you were confirmed. Your face on the press hoardings, the sinister headlines, would stir up thoughts of what you must have been guilty of, mixed up in, and who you are.

Your murder would not lead to a declaration of crisis or a call to find those responsible for it. Instead, it would be followed by conversations about the failure of integration, parental responsibility, the militarization of our suburbs, and there'd be politicians using the murder as a stick with which to drive home their own agenda.

You would not be considered an innocent child.

James Baldwin says: 'I know how you watch as you grow older, and it's not a figure of speech, the corpses of your brothers and your sisters pile up around you. And not for anything they have done. They were too young to have done anything.'

When for the first time you became fully visible to the public, you'd confirm the generally held fantasy about the nature of the threat facing every Swede, their life and existence, and the nation as a whole. You'd be regarded as culpable for your own death. The murder of you is to be regarded as a suicide.

The criminalization of a murdered child is the outcome of the series of processes constructed for this very purpose.

Judith Butler, the professor of literature and gender studies, argues that the political and media discourse dehumanizes certain people by attaching a debt of blame to them, a stigma that makes them ungrievable, and makes their killing unproblematic. She writes that by constructing and maintaining conceptions of who should be considered a normative human being and who shouldn't, one creates a narrative which, for instance, might be used to justify the waging of global war by the USA. One establishes a nationalistic norm for how an American looks and acts (and, by inference, does *not* look and act). In the same way we create *Swedishness*. To preserve the illusion of innocence of the Swede, it's crucial to have people like you depicted as perpetrators – or basically just avoid you being seen at all. The term used by Butler is 'make invisible'. She means that because you can't be seen and don't really exist, you're not real, which ultimately means you couldn't have died. The violence committed against you never took place. Or, to put it another way: you were stillborn. Nothing in the world, no government authorities, no integration projects, no crime mitigation measures, social services, basketball trainers, could have done anything to stop your predestined murder.

The terrible and predictable moment when someone of your own age who looks like you and lives in identical circumstances points a pistol at your head and pulls the trigger initiates the strange process of your coming alive for the very first time in the public space. While at the same time, by being presented in this way, you are turned into the very personification of evil. None of your privations, dreams, failures, thoughts or emotions – the things that make you a human being, with which other people can identify – are attached to your illusory features. You are devoid of spirit.

The Swedish self-image, its exceptionalism, the grandiose concept of ourselves as living in the foremost of all civilizations, the most illuminated and egalitarian of all nations, does not chime very convincingly with these child murders. The murdered children must therefore be refashioned into something else; not children, not humans. The murders have to be kept quiet, repressed, reinterpreted. They cannot be mourned in society as the tragedies they are. What I am trying to get at, Elijah, is that you could die; you could die without the majority of your countrymen giving a shit about your mutilated corpse. One imagines how you might be found by a passer-by who, after a certain amount of alarm, would note that you were a *blatte*, which would create a certain reassurance by triggering associations with the dominant narrative of murdered young *blattes*. The passer-by would realize that your death was no coincidence; you must have been involved in a cycle of violence, into which you had entered quite voluntarily, and which had led to your *self-inflicted* death. After this the police would be called and they would reach the same conclusion. Next, the ambulance would be called and they would reach the same conclusion. Journalists would arrive, also reaching the same conclusion. And then, finally, they'd report on the event in a language that would lead us all to the same conclusion.

33

We haven't heard anything from Abbe or Josef in over a month. There are reasonable grounds for suspicion against Abbe for aggravated robbery. It happened just a few days after we last met on that day in Rosengård. He's been moved from his family home to a young offenders' institution, so he's almost impossible to contact now. He can forget about training to make the national youth team. Apparently, Josef has also been moved into secure accommodation. When it happened or for what exact reason I don't know, you're the one who told me about it. I've been aware of him smoking weed and hanging out with older boys, and the training sessions with the team have become more and more sporadic. But I was unaware that he'd moved away from his father and Malmö. I can't bear to think about it.

You came home at 5 p.m. from a trip to Denmark. You'd played a top team. On the way back over the bridge you called me, joyfully hollering.

'We won, Nick!' you shouted. 'We won by fifty-four to fifty-two! And I scored as many points as our opponents.'

'What, you scored fifty-two points?' I asked.

'Yeah!' you shouted. 'Crazy, isn't it? It would have been even more knockout if I'd scored them all!'

We celebrated your heroic deed with double portions at Chicken Cottage. Our thoughts were constantly with Abbe and Josef; the atmosphere was muted. Afterwards we took a walk past People's Park, where we bumped into Carlos. He'd just come back from Peru, where he'd said his farewells to his father, who'd passed away. His face was heavy with sleeplessness.

'It's the feelings, brother,' he said gloomily. 'They're caught up inside. I can't take having them there.'

We stood by the pond next to Olof Palme's memorial stone. It was covered in bird shit. Behind the trees, in the park where families with children would sit on blankets, there were raucous men's voices. The alcoholics had arrived. You withdrew slightly, ended up in conversation with two young men a short distance away. One of them seemed high, I noted in the corner of my eye. He moved his body jerkily and stiffly, and he spoke too loudly. Then he turned around, said something, and pointed at me. You started walking back towards me.

'That guy behind me wants to talk to you, Nick,' you whispered when you came forward. 'He says you used to take him for basketball. He seems a bit fucked up. Scars all over his face.'

My heart was leaping in my chest as I drew closer to the men. They were about the same height as me, but young, twenty years old. If they tried anything, I had Carlos with me, we'd take them.

The guy with the cut face was called Petar. Sure enough I'd trained him when he was younger. The scars were fresh. Blue stitches stuck out like hairs from his skin. He'd been cut on his forehead, at an angle across his nose, lower lip and cheek.

'Hey, Nick,' he said. 'Remember me?'

He offered his hand. I gripped it. He wanted to embrace me but I kept my arm extended, stiff. I didn't want him too close.

'Course I recognize you,' I said. 'What the hell happened to you?'

'It was this dude,' he said, letting go of my hand, spitting at the gravel. 'I was playing Jack Vegas. Then he stood next to me, told me what to do and all, how I should play. I got pissed, told him: Clear off. Then he took a knife and stabbed me in the face. He was that sort of cunt. 'Cos he stabbed me from the side when I couldn't see him. We ended up on the floor and he stabbed and stabbed. And we had a fight. And yeah . . . You still play basketball?'

As we were leaving the park you told me he'd lied to me. He'd told you all about gang conflicts, people who were after him because of business, and so on. He said he'd been put away for attempted murder and only just released. 'But I could see he wasn't real, Nick,' you said. 'He just talked a lot of shit. You can see right off if someone's real.'

I looked at you ambling along with your little elk strides. You had snot coming out of one nostril, and your rucksack was thumping against your butt.

'What the hell do you know about being real, you little shit?' I said and gave you a gentle shove.

You laughed. 'I know a fair amount about being real, Nick,' you said, and put your hands in your pockets. 'I know a lot of stuff you don't even know anything about.'

34

Sometimes you ask if I think we would have been friends if we were the same age. I tell you: 'Yeah, I think so, because we've got basketball and hip hop in common.'

I'm lying.

You're not a bad kid. But you're always probing for your friends' sore points, and you press them. You can be hard work, violent and a bad friend. I wouldn't have wanted a pal like that.

No, let me rephrase that. I wouldn't have wanted to be a friend of yours, Elijah, because you're a bully. When I took you, Abbe and Josef to the basket at the far corner of the sports hall it wasn't only to disarm you and keep you away from hostile adults, but also to keep you away from other children, whom you were harassing.

All of my life, in every situation I have been involved in with other people, even as an adult, I've felt stupid. Stupid as in unintelligent, turgid, untalented, ill-informed, uneducated, clumsy, out of place, incompetent.

My body has been my big asset: I have had the ability to run, jump, carry and throw things, wrestle, dribble. But my intellect, on the other hand, my inner world of thoughts and emotions, has not been all there.

As a child, my future professional direction was obvious: manual work. I can't think of a single adult who ever said to me: 'You're smart, you could study and have a career, go far.' No – not even my mother encouraged me to study.

In senior school I was placed with 'students who have some difficulty with mathematics'. One of the teachers expressed herself in those terms when she informed us about our selection. It was not in any way unfair. I realized that from the very first day, when I, with the other carefully selected drongos – Amir, Danne, Veronica, Mille, Lukaz – showed up in the classroom.

We called ourselves the morons' class. Partly to make a joke of the fact that we'd been categorized as idiots. And partly to take the edge off the invective that was bound to follow.

In my head there was only space for things that demanded a very minimum of mental activity. I only thought about and cared about sport, music, American films and TV series, my friends, girls, clothes and stuff I wanted but did not have. To everything else – really, everything else – I was utterly unreceptive. And given that school was a place for everything else, it was not a place for me. If it weren't for the fact that my older brother had bunked out of school in year 9 and was then institutionalized, because he was such an unruly kid, which had broken Mum's heart, then I would have been the unruly kid who bunked out of school and broke my mother's heart.

Apart from that there were few similarities between me and my brother. The thing that set us apart most of all was without a doubt his high level of intelligence. He was exceptionally gifted. One headmaster told my mother that he was the smartest student in the whole school. Despite it all, he was eager to learn, he read books and was constantly searching for new knowledge. I remember the atmosphere around the dinner table – my brother and Mum involved in lively conversations. I sit at the short side of the table watching them, their tongues and mouths moving as they toss words back and forth. They talk, brag, engage in debate. I try to follow what they're saying. But it's useless. They might as well be talking in another language.

In addition to all this, my brother was courageous. One night he came home with cuts on his face, his body shaking. He nodded at me to follow him into his room. He told me in a tremulous voice how he and his mates had just run into a violent man. My brother said that he realized the danger they were in, he moved out of the man's field of vision, got out a baseball bat, and whacked it as hard as he could against the man's head. There was no sense of regret in his voice. His eyes glittered with pride. He'd exceeded himself, done the right thing even though he was frightened.

No one had less respect for grown-ups than my older brother. He did not view grown-ups as unassailable. If anyone fucked with him, there were consequences. He fought with tough guys. He constructed home-made arms from bangers and metal pipes.

He taught me how to fight. He told me to hit people in

157

the face. He said if you didn't hit people in the face, you were just a pussy. I hit Zeki and Kasper in the face as hard as I could. I sat on top of Zeki in the sports hall at the youth centre, kicked him as he was lying there and thumped his head against the floor. I hit Katarina in the face because she'd called me a *spagge* – a spick. I hit the recently arrived Kurdish boy in the face and then pressed sand into his mouth. I was given a beating by Karl, from Klippan, whose dad was a racist. And I took a beating from Jacob, who was both younger and shorter than me. Jacob had heard that I'd punched Katarina, and he'd seen me acting up as if I were the king of the playground. He bided his time. Jacob had a father, he was primally strong, and he lacked any need to assert himself. I'd been avoiding him because he had the ability to see right through me. He knew I was a coward. I imagine his satisfaction when, with a sharp blow like a whip-lash across my nose, he turned my smug smirk into pleading yells. Jacob took no pleasure in it as he looked down on me from above. His rotating fists hit me so hard that I had a concussion. He completed his task. Imposed justice.

I wasn't up to scratch. I always knew that. The ideals of the street fighter were never within reach for me. Or, as my brother put it, by nature I was a pussy.

Beyond the fact that my brother was violent, beyond the fact that he attacked those who were weak, he still had integrity. It's no contradiction. He never let himself be intimidated. One would not be wrong in asserting that he partially disavowed himself from his own humanity by stirring up violence in others. But by putting up resistance and not letting himself be pushed around, by throwing his punches for dear life, even at grown-ups, I'd like to think that he was protecting the core of his own being. They couldn't get at him.

Until he met with judgement.

One day my brother passed some boys who were playing football on a gravelled pitch. He told one of them to pass him the ball and, when he wasn't obeyed, he ran up to the boy and assaulted him. I remember the prosecutor describing the assault in detail, how after all the kicks he received the boy was peeing blood. Mum was utterly ashamed of herself, she said, when we stood in the hall putting on our best clothes before setting off to the City Court. My memories from there are some of the darkest of my life. We walk though bare white corridors and step into the courtroom. All eyes are on us as we sit down on our chairs, Mum and I, with my brother in the booth in front of us. Everything is cold: the atmosphere, people's eyes, the agitated voice of the prosecutor.

In that moment I hated my brother. I hoped they'd punish him. That he should sit there in the booth, eating their shit. *Damn little fucker*, I thought. He always had to ruin our lives. Mum always crying. And now we sat here before a group of strangers who hated us. Mum couldn't even look at him. She turned her neck like a bird, looking one way and then another. I followed the process with care, focusing on my brother as he sat there in the booth which was so clearly made for bigger, older bodies. Only his head stuck out at the top, his big, brown, water-combed pudding-bowl haircut.

My brother smiled sarcastically and wanted to seem tough, but the judge roared: 'You can wipe that smile off your face! Do you understand what you've done?'

The animosity in the courtroom was palpable, heavy to inhale. My brother looked so small. I'd always seen him as hard and invincible. But he wasn't. He was a little shit. Just like me. But over the course of the trial something happened inside of me. The hatred that I had focused on my brother was turned towards all the others. And when I say all the others, I really do mean all the others. Not just the grown-ups in the hall who wanted to crush him, and humiliate us, but all grown-ups. Society as a whole. The whole world.

Soon after, my brother was sent to a home for youth offenders and young people with drug problems. We visited him at the facility. The first time he was in a good mood. He didn't complain, everything was flowing pretty well. 'But the inmates here are morons,' he said. 'You can't talk to any of them, or have a normal conversation. It's about as interesting as talking to a wall. They're so fucking slow.'

That's what bothered him, I remember, as opposed to the violence hanging in the air, the fights in the communal room, the tasteless food, the narrow beds and the cramped space, or being away from Mum.

He didn't even complain about the warders. Later it emerged that the warders were drug abusers themselves. Weirdos and criminals. But that wasn't so bad either, I understood when we spoke. They could have been murderers, the whole bunch of them, as long as they saw him, hugged him, and told him he was good enough. He didn't say this in so many words. But that's what he meant. He only told me that the warders were a bunch of cunts. Which meant that he understood they didn't care about him, weren't interested in how he was feeling or how he was developing, and weren't watching his back. The only person who backed him, loved him, and who he loved back, was Mum. I can't say what I felt for my brother. The only thing I can say is that our relationship was, and is, complicated. It's difficult to love a person who torments you, who keeps you at a distance, disappoints you. A person you would like to love more than anyone else, but can't bring yourself to and aren't even allowed to.

With my brother at the facility, life became more harmonious and predictable. Mum knew where he was, and although she couldn't know what was going on or whether he was actually being rehabilitated, he was someone else's responsibility. He was in a place where concerns about violence, or him coming to harm, or the police calling to say that he was dead, no longer hung over her.

Not long before he was sent away the police called to say that my brother had been involved in a car accident. I was in my room when Mum answered the telephone, and I could hear by her voice that something was wrong. My brother and his friend had stolen a car. The police caught on to them and were quickly in pursuit. My brother's friend put his foot down, skidded across lawns and footpaths, the sirens just behind them. They drove into a residential area and crashed the car right into a house. The car was a write-off, the police said to Mum. It may have been their condescending and lecturing tone, their dramatic choice of words, the shame, combined with a terror of what might have happened, that made her explode. I can't remember what she shouted at them. Only that she was livid, wiping the floor with them. And that, when I rushed into the kitchen, I found her standing there pale as a sheet with the telephone in her hand.

'He's okay,' she said in a low voice while her eyes filled with tears. 'He's been in a car accident, but he's okay. He's okay.'

She told me that the police, as they walked up to the smoking vehicle with their pistols drawn, had been certain that those inside the car must be dead, that no one could have survived such an impact. And then what they found inside were two slim-as-sticks youths wedged into the compressed front seat. If they hadn't been so small, they would have been dead.

Was that why I flinched when you sent me that picture of yourself at the wheel of that car?

After two years my brother came home again. In his eyes, which before had been rebellious, there was now mainly just emptiness and darkness. We stood in the kitchen all three of us. Mum was yelling and crying. I was crying too, and my brother stood in silence, leaning against the veranda door, with a cigarette in his mouth. When Mum ran away into the bedroom I took over.

'You fucking idiot. You've ruined everything! Don't you understand what you've done!'

Before, I wouldn't have dared shout at him like that. But now he took it. He listened and kept quiet. Something clicked inside for him. As if he only then realized what he'd done, how much we cared. The next day he broke things off with his usual crowd, promising betterment. He started hanging out with me and my friends and became a part of our gang. I didn't like it. He occupied space, space that was mine. But he was in recovery, everyone noticed that. I couldn't let my small-mindedness fuck it all up for him now.

35

Then came that telephone call from our grandfather. 'Your mother has cancer.' It might take a couple of weeks, or a month or so. But Mum was going to die.

We rushed over to the hospital, stormed into her room, and wept in each other's arms. 'I know it's terrible, my darlings,' she said, 'but there's not a whole lot we can do about it. We just have to accept the situation as it is. Our remaining time together is going to be the best time we ever had.'

But it wasn't. Mum's body broke down. The months went by, her gradual sickening became routine. None of it seemed particularly sad. When I graduated from secondary school, a few months before Mum died, she was bedbound. Being upright was potentially life-threatening for her. Even if she went to the toilet she could collapse under her own weight and die from her fall.

My grades were unfinished and worthless. But it was a significant event; I was the first ever member of our family to graduate secondary school. 'It has to be celebrated,' said Mum, lying there wrapped up in her duvet, her face radiant with pride.

We decided that I should celebrate my graduation with friends in a premises we'd hire close to where we lived. And that later we'd have sandwich cake together, just the two of us sitting on her bed, talking about my future. The atmosphere peaked when the flatbed truck swung into the parking area outside where the party was being held. I had a garland of flowers around my neck and my student cap on my head. My friends were there, a couple of relatives had come, we laughed and sang. Then, suddenly, I saw Mum in the throng, tiptoeing towards me as if walking on broken glass. She was wearing that ugly grey coat she had for special occasions, and she'd combed her thin, close-cropped grey hair. I had time to reflect that this would be the last time I saw her all dressed up and looking nice – for something as meaningless as my secondary school graduation. I hurried over and embraced her.

'Careful!' she whimpered as I put my arms around her. She pushed me away.

'Sorry, Mum,' I said. Right at the end, hugging was too painful.

And then she slowly grew worse. Sometimes I was overcome by the knowledge that she would soon be gone, which made me collapse in despair. This happened on maybe three occasions. But otherwise, there were no emotions.

Instead, I felt a growing need to hurt my brother. *Your chance will come,* I told myself. *Have some patience, the moment is almost here.*

* * *

We walked through the greenery outside the hospice. My brother wept. I consoled him. Soon there would just be the two of us, we said. We had to promise to stick together, whatever happened. We were the only ones left.

We sat on either side of the hospital bed, holding Mum's hands. Granddad sat on a chair next to my brother. His eyes were bloodshot, he was as clipped and closed as ever. His firstborn, Mum's oldest sister, had died when she was ten. Now that his youngest was about to die, he would outlive two of his three daughters.

Mum wasn't much bigger than a ten-year-old where she lay almost upright in her bed. She breathed with a wheezing sound. Five seconds between breaths, ten seconds, fifteen, thirty. Her cranium was full of veins under her velvety soft whirls of hair. Her mouth was distended. Her eyes like small globes in their hollows.

Mum died at one in the morning. I stood up and took my coat off the hook, then turned back to look at her. I tried to take it all in. She was so incredibly skinny. Emaciated, dried up, withered as a stick. We were met in the corridor by two nurses. One of them held out her arms, burst into tears and hugged me hard.

The day after, we were once again standing in front of Mum's body, my brother and me. They'd spruced her up, opened her eyes and powdered her skin. Coming to see the body was just something you did, I'd been told. If not customary, then at least a good tradition. 'See it as a moment of spiritual contemplation,' they said. 'A last moment with your mother. You can talk to her if you like. Whisper something that she would have liked to hear. A secret just between the two of you.'

God, no. Nothing could feel more unnatural to me. Mum was dead. Her shell couldn't be spoken to, my voice wouldn't be heard. If I did any of that stuff, I'd hate myself.

We stood by the side of the bed, looking at her. Her facial expression was mild, free of pain. She looked like people do when they've just died and been taken care of by the nursing staff, so that we, the next of kin, can say: *She looked so peaceful. At least she didn't feel any pain.* After our visit, after this moment of spiritual contemplation, she'd be wheeled into the corridor, out of the hospice entrance, and into the nearby crematorium. There, she'd be lifted off the bed, placed in the oven, and then go up in flames.

Mum was unsentimental. I liked that about her. No whining, just straight to the point. For instance, that desperate evening at the hospital when she said that we had to accept the situation, make the best of it. Mum had snorted disdainfully at the thought of being buried. 'The only purpose of graves is to make those who are left behind have a bad conscience. Just burn my remains. I'll still be there in your memories.'

Next stop the crematorium, I thought. *Still wearing her clothes. Just the way she is, right now.*

But why the hell was she wearing my T-shirt? I looked at it. The T-shirt was white, with a colourful basketball motif across the chest. It was mine. I liked wearing it when I was training. Mum often borrowed my clothes, which was fair enough. She never bought anything for herself, she always walked around in the same old rags because she spent her money on us. But now she knew she was going to *die* and her body was going to be *cremated* – with my T-shirt on. It had all been pre-arranged. Wasn't it bloody inconsiderate and self-centred of her not to think about it earlier, not to take off my T-shirt in advance? I went into a panic. I wanted to yell at her, grab the fabric and pull the T-shirt over her head, taking back what was mine. *Shit, Mum! Fucking shit!*

My anger subsided. I had a notion. I wanted to see whether I could catch her remote gaze. I looked into her protruding, clouded eyes. I leaned forward. A feeling came over me. Slowly and deliberately, I pulled down her eyelids. This was my allotted task, I felt in that moment. To close my mother's eyes. That's what one did. I'd seen it in films. Her eyeballs flexed softly under my fingertips; I pushed down the eyelids to shut them. But when I took my hand away they opened and went back to their original position. What the hell? I did it again. Slid my fingers down over the eyelids, closed them, moved my hand away, but once more they opened. It scared me. I stepped back, a chill running through my body. I'd crossed a line. I felt this in my whole being. I was terribly ashamed. I hated myself.

The last few months in the apartment were hell. Mum had been a moderating force between me and my brother, but now that she was gone a collision was unavoidable. My brother got me worked up, pushed at my boundaries, triggering an attack. I kept myself calm and gathered my anger inside. My attack, once it happened, had to be resolute.

I knew that much. No hesitation, no fear. Fear would stymie my movement. I had to feel hatred. Pure hatred.

We were in the kitchen. My brother was stirring a pot, in his usual bad mood. He usually took care of the cooking. He was good in the kitchen, but it took him an age. And he blew his own trumpet about it.

'Shit, this is going to be really nice . . . You know what it is? No, you don't, do you? You never had food like this,' he said. 'You lot, you and your boys, you only eat crap. It's got to be fresh produce, minimalist dishes. But you don't get it. 'Cos you only eat shit. I've seen what you put way. Bread and sauces, pre-packaged foods and crap. Your bodies are rotting from the inside, you know that? No, you don't. You don't know anything.'

'Shut your mouth and finish what you're doing,' I said. 'Anyone can cook if they take four hours over it.'

'No,' he said. 'Not anyone. You wouldn't get anywhere with it even if you had a lifetime. I've seen you, don't forget that. I know how your brain works, how little space you got in there. You can't even make quick-boil macaroni without turning it into porridge. And that's why you're shit, and you eat shit.'

'Fuck you,' I said.

'Man, fuck you,' he said. 'Go and eat your dry sandwiches instead, you're not having any of this food.'

'Fuck you,' I said again.

He stopped and turned to me.

'If you say "fuck you" one more time, I'll beat the crap out of you.' He continued stirring the pot.

'Fuck you,' I said and stood up.

Quick as a flash he picked up the fork from the kitchen counter and hurled it at me. I dodged it and then advanced, grabbed hold of his body, and threw him to the floor. He was on his feet in an instant, charging towards me. Then he stopped. His face was red. He yelled from the depths of his being: 'I'll kill you! I'll kill you!'

He snorted, leaning in like a wrestler, without moving forward an inch. Then he stormed out of the kitchen and slammed the door to his room. I heard him thumping the walls, roaring, tearing things down so they hit the floor. I stood there in the kitchen, shaking from the surge of adrenaline. I felt happy, ecstatic.

Afterwards came both sorrow and a deep anxiety. This was what he had, I thought to myself. His violence and his superiority. And I was also what he had, his younger brother, someone he could boss around. I'd let him down. I'd shifted the order of things, switched roles with him. What would happen now? My anxiety turned into terror. I wanted to make amends. Run into his room, fall on my knees, apologize a thousand times.

36

It was my older brother who introduced me to hip hop. First there was gangster rap in the early nineties, then savvier hip hop, street rap, boom bap from New York. He was actually as uninterested in politics as me. No one spoke about politics. The fact that it was wedged into the music, as integral a feature of hip hop as swearing, was not something I thought about or was even aware of. But I felt that the rappers, unlike me, had taken control of their daily existence, their bodies. Even though they were surrounded by violence and danger, threatened by poverty and harassed by the police. They didn't let anyone fuck with them. They were free. They were suffused with anger, sometimes hatred. And the lyrics reverberated in me.

I loved how rappers with pen and paper as sword and shield went out into the world, but I also loved everything else: the romanticization of violence, the fetishization of weapons, the homophobic sentiments, the misogyny. I loved the lyrics that so bluntly and in minute detail accounted for the predicament of Black Americans, the predicament of Latinos, or the predicament of the underclass or working-class *blattes* in Sweden.

Hip hop became my entrance gate to literature. The rapper Ras Kass had stolen the author Eldridge Cleaver's book title *Soul on Ice* for his record and I wanted to know why. It was a huge reading experience. Cleaver had written the book in a cell in Folsom State Prison in 1965, and it was uncompromising, virulent, raw, ideologically razor-sharp, absolutely close to reality, and as well-written and smart as any book by William Faulkner or Marguerite Duras. In addition, as it turned out, Cleaver was a leading figure in the Black Panther Party – a writer and intellectual activist – which was the greatest thing anyone could be, as I saw it.

And yet there was something in the text that grated. Cleaver kept himself within strict emotional boundaries to avoid exposing any weak or vulnerable side to himself. Projecting himself as unyielding, hard, manly, confessing that he'd raped women, that he hated gays and was uneducated – none of this was problematic for him. These were the same ideals and shortfalls that I'd found in rap music. But the actual human being, the one who was pathetic, had panic attacks, cried himself to sleep, worried about his children, had sex with men, was paranoid and stressed to pieces by death threats and attempted murders, self-pitying and insufficient and suffering from erectile dysfunction – where was he in all this?

But my interest in literature – protest literature, Afro-American literature – had been awakened. And there was a welter of authors offering the depth that I was missing: James Baldwin, bell hooks, Toni Morrison, John Edgar Wideman. And then, as time went by: Arundhati Roy,

Simone de Beauvoir, Annie Ernaux, Primo Levi, Aleksandr Solzhenitsyn. Later, as if there had to be a circumnavigation of the earth prior to discovering the Swedish authors: Vilhelm Moberg, Stig Dagerman, Selma Lagerlöf, Märta Tikkanen, Ivar Lo-Johansson, Hjalmar Söderberg. And later still: Sven Lindqvist, Kristian Lundberg, Susanna Alakoski, Andrzej Tichý, Johannes Anyuru.

It was the classics that made Sweden accessible to me, that told me about the cold, austere, rural and in every way bleak and grey landscape. Yet at the same time it was still the incredibly attractive Sweden of the past – the land that was still here. It was history and exploration at the same time, as if the fairy tales of my early childhood were actually true. How I would have benefitted from this in my early teenage years, I often thought. It had made me realize that the land out there beyond the apartment blocks, in every possible way, also belonged to me.

37

The largest of the three buildings that make up Malmö's City Library, known as Ljusets kalender (the Calendar of Light), has glass facades that reach to a height of some twenty metres. The main reading room faces onto Slottsparken on two sides. Through the window, from the table where I was sitting, I could see the multicoloured playground apparatus of Sagolekplatsen (the Fairy Tale Playground), also the pond and the areas of greenery. Everything was grey with rain and mist. Twenty minutes earlier I'd stood in the entrance vestibule, waiting for you. We had talked about and planned this visit for a long time; it was going to be your first one ever. We were going to stroll around the shelves, taking down whatever books took our fancy, reading about the writers on the sleeves. We were going to borrow the book you picked for yourself, and then read it out loud in the evenings. But then, five minutes after the time we'd arranged, you sent an SMS to let me know you weren't coming, you were still in the sports hall.

Okay, Elijah, I thought. *I couldn't give a damn. If you want to stay stupid and uneducated for the rest of your life, it's entirely up to you.*

The reading room was packed. Everywhere I saw the tops of people's heads, where they sat with their eyes looking down at books, computers, notepads – their futures. They were young, probably students the whole lot of them. An inscrutable bunch.

To one side ahead of me sat a young man with headphones on his head, which were as big as sound mufflers. On the chair to the right sat another young man, also with headphones, lost in a book. Opposite, with her back towards the hall and gazing out towards the park, sat a young woman, weeping.

Why she was weeping I don't know. She had sat like that for fifteen minutes.

Her face was expressionless, nothing about her conveyed sorrow. The tears just ran, down her cheeks and under her chin.

I leaned forward and made myself as small as I could. Pretended to write something, with my face unnaturally close to the screen. The woman couldn't be sure that I had seen her, I thought. She may have suspected that I had, but she couldn't be sure. I grew irritated. Not having the good judgement to withdraw so that others didn't have to be bothered by her bawling was offensive. Bawling was something one did privately and alone; you didn't deal with sorrow in the public eye. Then I felt empathy for her. Or at least sympathy. Is it the election, I thought? Is that why she's sad? Has she just noticed what's happening in her country? Is she crying because we've all sunk so low? And she doesn't want to be a part of it?

*   *   *

There came a thudding sound from the window of the great hall. It sounded as if someone had bashed their elbow or slammed their head into the glass. An everyday sound, which, at first, I didn't pay much heed to. But I'd heard it before.

The sound is made by birds flying into the facade, being crushed against the invisible wall of glass. Some are killed by the impact or knocked out and killed when they hit the ground. Others survive, flap their wings, and continue on their way. A few are alive as they fall, yet they meet a cruel fate. I see their flailing wings beat as they hurtle through the air, then crash-land in the gravel in a cloud of feathers and dust. The minutes draw out as they lie there thrashing. It's an unpleasant sight. And I know how it ends. Their mortal struggle attracts attention. Other birds flock around the dying ones, also related species. Impatiently they skip and hop and glare with jerking neck movements. And, once the fallen has died, they feast on the carrion. Their gorging is violent and cannibalistic. Feathers fly through the air, there's an echo of chattering and shrieking, beaks penetrate the shredded flesh, turn up towards the sky then gulp down the food.

Most of the birds flying into the glass panes of Malmö's City Library are residents – magpies, pigeons, rooks. But some are migrants on their way out. Once, a large goose flew into a window on the second floor. I was sitting right there. In the corner of my eye I saw a shadow approaching at high speed, and then, before I'd had time to react, the goose had flown into the glass. I jumped and turned my head just as it fell into the flower bed. For a long time, filled with loathing and disgust, I looked at the lifeless body. What a bloody waste. Simple measures could have prevented its death. If they'd fixed black bird stickers at the tops of the windows, or even avoided constructing a building out of transparent glass, it would have survived.

I looked at the body lying in the brown soil. It seemed to be sleeping. Its heart had stopped beating. But when the wind blew through its feathered suit, the goose drew breath once more.

My unease lingered, much stronger this time than when I'd seen other birds dying.

No fairy tale had ever made a stronger impression on me than *The Wonderful Adventures of Nils.*

When Eva, my primary schoolteacher, read to us from the book, I remember how Sweden, in the slightly archaic language of Selma Lagerlöf, expanded and became understandable to me, spread out like a wonderland under my feet. My own experience of Sweden was grey – grey concrete, grey skies, grey people. But here it flourished in myriad colours. Here, there were infernal hollows, copper mines and labyrinthine passages; here were animals, forests and rivers that could talk; here the mountains soared high and cut through the clouds; here the landscapes were so multifarious that in one moment one would be looking out over a far-ranging, snow-covered expanse, only to be plodding

---

* *The Wonderful Adventures of Nils* by Selma Lagerlöf is an early twentieth-century classic novel, in which a boy sees the whole of Sweden from the back of a goose.

through mysterious, forested mountains in the next, where there were beings that humans should stay well clear of. Trolls and mylings, witches and giants, dragons and dryads; here were castles and sun-drenched gardens with fruit trees and straight roads studded with rows of willows; here were windmills and impressive stubbled fields and billowing, golden, yellow fields of rape and silvery streams; here bloody wars had been fought; here were villages that looked like fortresses, abandoned, crumbled gates and walls that had stood there since the medieval age.

Why do I feel a resistance inside when I write like this? About Sweden as beautiful, a place stirring the imagination – right out of the fairy tales.

Because it's true.

I have seen the land with my own eyes. Sweden is not just our walk from the flat to the square in Möllan, basketball practice in sweaty sports halls, hanging out in the park with Abbe and Josef in the spring, the boredom around where we live. It's so much more than that. And I would like you to be able to see it, Elijah.

You, like most of the others, don't believe that the fairy tales belong to you. The children in the gnomic mountains don't look like you. *Mio, My Son* is not you. *Blattes* do not roam around in John Bauer's forests. And you have nothing in common with the farm boy, Nils Holgersson, who learns to love nature, and whose story people love so much.

Isn't that how you see it? Isn't this the sort of thing you're told?

But what if it's precisely the other way round, Elijah? What if the way you see yourself in this land, the alienation you've been saddled with and have absorbed into your being, is the great lie of your life? And that, in fact, the rows of fairy tales in the children's reading section and the young adult shelves in Malmö's City Library are actually talking about your life? What if you are Nils Holgersson?

You'd laugh about that. You'd be embarrassed, maybe even slightly offended. You can't afford to think like that. It's too risky. It hurts too much. You have to ridicule the very suggestion of it.

But think about it now: what human being could be more like Nils Holgersson than you?

You're both boys from Skåne. You grew up in difficult, deprived circumstances. You're fourteen years old. You both grew up as only children. You have few friends. Both of you are often up to no good and you can behave bloody abominably. You're both anxious and extroverted. Products of your environment.

Can't you see that yourself? You're one and the same, you and Nils. He's you and you're him. Two lads from the south of Sweden.

Right now, you're in the middle of a life-changing journey. You're standing on the edge of the new, and you've dared to make the leap. You're subjected to trials. You break down, you're alone, and you long for home. But when the world opens, something also opens in you. In your meeting with others, you also meet yourself.

You're perched up there now, on the back of a wild goose,

just like Nils. You clamber onto it. You feel the thrill in your stomach as it takes off, rises towards the sky. Beneath you lie the concrete buildings of Nydala, the heart-formed map of Malmö, quickly broken up by the clouds. You sail away across the immensity. Skåne's unequalled beauty: patchwork quilts and lakes, small villages and towns, roads forming arteries across the landscape and connecting us all.

It's yours, Elijah. Sweden is yours.

38

It was a normal Friday. I was cycling along Södra Skolgatan towards the apartment, where you were, when I heard three gunshots. It was about midday. The shots were fired in rapid succession, echoing with a metallic ring between the buildings. People started yelling in panic. I was on my way back to pick you up. We were going to pack our bags and head off to the sports hall.

When the racist serial killer Peter Mangs was on the loose in Malmö, hardly a day went by without newspaper headlines: **New shooting in Malmö**. Malmö residents were being randomly targeted – in their homes, cars, at bus stops, the gym, mosque, on their bicycles heading home after football practice.

Mangs did not only shoot at Black or brown people. To create chaos and divert people's attention, arouse hatred of *blattes* and the multicultural society, and start his much longed for race war, he also shot at buildings, street signs, buses and police stations.

Malmö became a ghost town. Suspicion spread among locals. The police, who couldn't imagine such a thing as a white terrorist, spent several fruitless months chasing down *blattes* to arrest. This was totally in accordance with Mangs' plans.

We had to shut down our work. Hundreds of kids were left without any leisure activities, and local facilities were left empty. Parents called in the evenings, crying, terrified that the bullets, which seemed to travel with the wind, would strike down their children. We went with the children to and from school, peering over our shoulders, into thickets and passing cars. We exhorted parents to do the same. Keep the children at home, we said. Away from windows. And if there is any way, leave the city until the thing that has taken possession of it has been displaced.

When we had finished training in the hall in the evening I sent you, Abbe and Josef home on your own. I felt guilty about it. It was irresponsible to socialize out of doors and to go to the sports hall. When you headed off I didn't know if I'd ever see you again.

The fear that you'd be hit by the arbitrary bullets was not irrational. Kamal, someone we both knew, was shot by Peter Mangs. He was sixteen years old, on his way home after a training session, cycling up a hill when Mangs turned up. The first shot hit him in the neck, throwing Kamal off the bicycle. Mangs stood over him as he lay there on the ground, still conscious, and emptied the chamber. Another four bullets hit Kamal: in the armpit, thigh, shinbone and forehead. The latter is still lodged in Kamal's head, in the groove between his brain lobes, impossible to remove surgically. He'll live with it for the rest of his life.

* * *

The screams and noise abated when I turned into Möllevångsgatan. On the corner by the 7–Eleven, two boys sat hunched against the cold, each with an ice cream and some Pokémon cards strewn across the asphalt. I stopped by Södra Förstadsgatan, looked left and right. Then kept cycling until I came to our entrance, where I parked the bike.

You were lying on the sofa with your mobile phone when I walked in, nodding at you as a greeting.

'Everything okay?' I asked, sitting down at the computer. There was a siren in the distance. I couldn't determine whether a police car or an ambulance.

'It's all good, brother,' you said in a muted voice. 'But something has happened, Nick. A really big thing.'

I came to attention. How could he already know about it?

'I talked to my coach today,' you went on. 'He thinks I'll make the national team. We'll find out in the next few days.'

'For real?' I said. I surfed the online edition of *Sydsvenskan*. There was nothing as yet about any shooting. I turned to you. 'That's amazing.'

'Yeah, but that means I have to have money this summer, Nick. 'Cos we're playing in Denmark and playing the German team as well. It's a big tournament. Like . . . if I'm picked for it.'

'We'll handle that,' I said. I turned off the computer and got off the chair. There were sirens coming from all directions now, patrol cars and ambulances. You looked towards the window, then at me.

'Yeah, but I don't want to jinx it,' you said superstitiously. 'Just think if I don't make it.'

'Of course you will,' I said. 'Why wouldn't you?'

I took your hand and hoisted you off of the sofa. 'Congratulations, brother!' I said and hugged you.

'Don't say that, Nick. What if we jinx it?'

We'd planned a ninety-minute session, but we stayed in the sports hall for three hours. From time to time I logged onto the net on my mobile. And then it started appearing. At first, the information was scant: Shooting in Möllevången. One person shot. Then more details: A man of about thirty. Shot several times. It wasn't clear whether the man had died. And there was no information that might give away his identity.

The training opened slightly tentatively. You weren't getting into the drills; you were vacant and distracted. It irritated me, and I urged you on. You grew sulky: 'Can't we kick off a bit soft?'

'The Germans are not going to go easy on you,' I said. 'You might as well get used to it.'

Craig joined in. He's a year older than you and a head taller, with long arms and fast hands. When you two play, you have a hard time rising to the challenge.

Craig turning up raised the stakes, stressed you, sharpened your focus. I made use of the situation. I thought to myself, *Shit, now you're going to get a thrashing.*

After the warm-up, which was pretty lax, we practised dribbling. We picked up the pace. The next element involved attacking moves from the wing, towards the basket with a single bounce of the ball. I hit you both hard across your

184

arms and upper bodies. Craig sucked it up. But you were close to tears.

Heavy-spiritedness, anger or ill humour are fuel for a good training session. I rarely flare up. Usually, we communicate in a conversational tone, and you have no problems getting motivated.

Children learn in different ways. Some by reading, others by watching, feeling, listening or testing something out, doing it. For you, it hardly makes any difference at all what I say. It's my movements that you watch. As if you are scanning them and incorporating them into your own self. Inexperienced coaches can't do much for you. It is hard for you to convert theory into practice. So I demonstrate and instruct, and you watch and imitate. In this way, through minute adjustments, hour after hour, year after year, your way of playing basketball – your body movements and your technique – have become almost identical to my own.

If you are in a good and harmonious mood, we rarely exceed the planned training time. At such times we warm up in a modest way, talk about anything other than basketball, enjoy being there in the sports hall, and this well-being means that the exercises are crap. Your approach becomes more like many of your teammates' perspective on their sporting activity: an easy-going indifference, basketball as a way of passing the time, as a social activity.

You're at your best when you train with tunnel vision, shutting out the surroundings, only watching the ball and the basket, and pushing yourself to the limit.

The last hour, which we usually spent head to head, was destined to go overboard. I decided to join in myself. 'Let's play one on one,' I said. 'One point wins the game, the winner stays at the basket. The one with the most wins at the end gets no push-ups. The runner-up gets 150. The third place gets 200.'

Immediately things turned aggressive. I made full use of my strength, shoved you out of the way and put the ball in the basket. Against Craig I used my speed to get past. I won one game after another.

Two more years I can dominate you, then no more. Soon you'll grow stronger and more self-confident. By that point I'll be likely to lose, and then I won't play you any more.

To provoke you, make you lose your focus, I talked rubbish.

'It's not supposed to be this easy to score,' I said. 'If you play like that against the Germans, they'll crush you.' And: 'If you can't even win against an old man, how are you going to make the national team?'

You were close to breaking point. Your face was red and your lower lip flecked with white foam. Whenever you attacked and were about to shoot, I struck your hands or gave you a slight push to make you miss. It sent you into a rage.

'Foul!' you screamed. 'That's a fucking foul, Nick!'

Afterwards you sat on the bench, sulking, your jersey soaked with sweat and your arms covered in scratches and red marks. You glared at me as I calmly slid the mop over the floor, then turned off the lights in the hall.

'Can we go and eat now or what?' you asked at last.

'Sure we can,' I said. 'But first I want my 200 push-ups.'

39

This afternoon, my colleague Rahim called to tell me about the man who was shot. Rahim said his name was Peyman, and then asked if I knew him. I didn't. Had never heard his name. And as soon as I said it and it sank in that Peyman was not someone I was familiar with, a weight eased off my shoulders. It was a weight I hadn't even realized I was carrying. In other words, I'd been tense and subconsciously fretting about it over the last twenty-four hours. It's a repetitive experience when one lives in Malmö: only once the anxiety eases off does one realize how much one has been occupied by it.

I often think that my relationship with the city is symbiotic. I've lived and worked here for so long, so many people and places have been meaningful to me, that my own well-being is inextricably bound to that of Malmö and its people.

If I hear news of a fire in some flat in Lindängen, where someone has died, I feel an anxiety inside. I may be able to push the event out of my conscious thoughts, but not until I've found out that the deceased is unknown to me does the tension release. Every time I get information of a young person dying, I react in the same way: I feel a knot tightening around my heart, a shock like icy water runs through my body, and then instinctively I press down hard to contain the anxiety that follows. I hold my breath and I wait. And when I finally hear who it was that died, the anxiety either breaks through my protective walls or I feel a sort of grim relief. Irrespective of which, I see before me the network of people and places that will be affected – friends and acquaintances, schools and associations, the local area where the tragedy played out. And, as a consequence of this: how will I take a position on the event on a personal and professional level? This is the thing. This fact of always having to take a position on the evil is unspeakably tiring. Whatever has happened – whether accidents, murders or flaring conflicts – the uncertain wait is often the worst thing of all, because it reanimates the ghosts of the past, and asks the question: will I lose once again?

Rahim was superficially acquainted with Peyman, but he didn't seem personally affected. He told me that Peyman had been shot in the leg, back and face. And that he'd survive. Several people had witnessed the event, and apparently the shooter made his getaway in the exact direction in which I was cycling.

Then he read my thoughts: it wasn't impossible that the murder attempt would lead to more violent actions, a spiral of vengeance, and that the area – in other words our local area – would become a hotspot. Bombs could be detonated, bullets whizz by, exactly where you spend your time.

No one I know is better informed than Rahim about

what's going down in Malmö. If anything happens, I immediately see his name on my display. Through his family and
his circle of acquaintances, his many years of fieldwork,
his insight into politics and bureaucracy combined with a
confidence-inspiring personality and his growing up in
Rosengård, he has a unique perspective on the city – who
controls what areas, who's running the market, what compet-
itors and upstarts there are, and where the risks of escalating
conflicts lie, and thereby who runs the risk of dying.

It's people like Rahim who are best placed to prevent
tragedies and move the city in a more positive direction. But
the white middle classes would never hire an underclass *blatte*
with strong local connections when an influential post came
up. Instead, he must go on working unseen. Putting out fires,
consoling survivors, scolding the authorities. And just being
crucial to what he describes as 'Malmö, occupied city'.

Rahim rails at friends, relatives and acquaintances about
what idiots they are not to use their organizational skills and
capacity for working under the radar, creating something
new out of nothing, building up their areas rather than just
being parasitic on them. He's talking to deaf ears and he
knows it. People laugh at him but with warmth, in just the
same way that he laughs at them. The same driving force,
the same attributes and contact networks that make him a
tip of the javelin in the social work of Malmö, also lift his
family into pre-eminence in its shady field.

'I get them,' he often says. 'They're idiots, but I get them.'

As for myself, I move further and further away from the
epicentre of all the conflicts. I'm less in the field these days.

But I can't distance myself from death. The young people who are dying are those that I once worked with. At that time, they were in secondary school. So when their faces turn up in the news, I know straight away who they are, and I'm thrown back in time. It's a dizzying experience. The faces looking back at me are older and hardened versions of the children I once knew. The children running towards me on the playground, throwing themselves into my arms, their faces beaming with happiness.

Now they are in the grey zone between childhood and adulthood, the age at which they can most easily be manipulated, and they find it most difficult to comprehend action and consequence. They want to assert themselves and they're forced into minefields in order to carry out jobs for those who are older. Planting bombs, shooting and being shot.

I have to endure a few more years of it. Then the number of familiar faces in the newspapers will slowly reduce, until they are all strangers.

For my field-working colleagues, such as Rahim, it's the opposite. They're fully engaged in building relationships with the future dead.

40

The winter when Charles was murdered there were another five murders in Malmö over a short period of time. A fifteen-year-old who took part in our activities, someone you'd played basketball with, was shot dead in the night on New Year's Eve, just a few days before the same fate befell Charles. Someone, who's not yet been arrested, took his opportunity, and shot the boy during the booming of the fireworks.

A ghostly mood once more descended over the city. The murder spree led to one of the biggest police operations in Swedish history. There were police everywhere. They stood posted on street corners, they tore past across pavements and streets in wailing patrol cars and vans. There was an auditory backdrop of helicopter rotor-blades. This time, no racist terror had triggered things. This was a case of a seething eruption of conflict between Malmö residents.

I'd never hated the city so much.

Others shared my frustration. Opportunists without any capacity for political analysis decided to organize a 'Demonstration Against Violence' in central Malmö. But their frustration and criticism weren't directed at the political leadership or the decades of development that had put

Malmö at the top of the list of unequal cities, with the highest proportion of poor people in Sweden – instead, they were addressing their ire at a diffuse group: the *criminals*.

With my arms crossed, I sat down in front of the computer and watched the livestream from Gustav Adolfs Plaza, the public square. The 'We Shall Overcome' mood was unbearable, even from a distance. Thousands of Malmö residents crowding together, chanting in unison, 'No criminals in our city!' and 'You're not welcome in our beloved Malmö.' Home-made banners fluttering in the wind: 'More hugs!' and 'The cycle of violence is broken with love.' It was like witnessing the beginnings of the brainwashing of a one-thousand-strong sect. And then something happened that broke the spell. Yelling voices were heard. The speaker grew silent and unsure. People anxiously looked around. A curious group made their way through the crowd. On the stage, the speaker, also the organizer of the event, once more began to speak. He gestured and shushed to get the spectators to focus on something other than the hecklers. But to no avail.

For this was reality that was paying them a visit. It was the murdered fifteen-year-old's family that had arrived. There was no message of love on their placards. Only enlarged photographs of a dead child. A child shot with five bullets, lying all swelled up on a hospital bed. A boyish face besmirched with blood, a small body connected to a respirator. People wolf-whistled and jeered. Irritation spread. Family members cried out their despair, wept with boundless sorrow. It was unacceptable. The evening was ruined.

192

I'd never hated Malmö so much.

Rahim called on the way home from the demonstration. 'You should have been there, Nick,' he said. 'Everyone was there. It was a good atmosphere.'

'Are you stupid or what?' I hissed. 'I can't even talk about it. It's exactly this total lack of respect and humility that's going to lead to even more murders. And makes the problems stay where they are. Don't you understand?'

Rahim said: 'Have it your way, be grumpy. We had a great time anyway.'

Three weeks later Rahim called in a state of near breakdown. Another murder had taken place, the final one that winter. A man of about forty had been shot to death in a park in Husie. The murder had been carefully planned. The victim had been lured to the spot and was sitting there waiting when someone came up and shot him several times.

Rahim's weeping made a grating sound down the line. And then he managed to say: 'He was my uncle, Nick. My uncle. The bastards got him.'

I listened. Cold inside.

'Terrible thing to hear, brother,' I said. 'Fuck, that's just terrible.'

I'd never hated Malmö so much.

41

The light flooded into the bedroom as you pushed the sliding door open. I quickly sat up and peered at you.

'Sorry, Nick,' you whispered. 'But I can't find the keys and I'm late for school.'

I turned my back towards you without saying anything, pulling the duvet up to cover my body.

'Nick, I'm sorry . . .' you said. 'But I really need the keys. I can't find them.'

You had my grey trousers on. Also my black hat and purple-orange scarf. In the draft behind you as you stepped into the room I caught the stink of a strong aftershave. My aftershave.

'They're under the letters on the shelf in the hall,' I muttered. 'Where they always are.'

'Aha, okay, nice.' You turned around. 'See you later!'

When you left, you forgot to lock the front door. You didn't slide the door back behind you. And now the hall light was glaring like a little sun. Burning through my eyelids. Anyway, my anger had stirred my pulse. So there was nothing for it but to get up. Go into the kitchen and put on the coffee. And confirm that you had ruined another day.

* * *

The following morning.

The light flowed into the bedroom when you pushed aside the sliding door. This time, only halfway. I understood at once what was happening, the item of news that you wanted to pass on.

'I made it, Nick!' you whispered loudly. 'I just had the mail. I made the national team! . . . Nick . . . You hear me? Hello? I made it, I said. I'm on the national team!'

'Congratulations, brother,' I mumbled, with my face in the pillow.

'Wicked, isn't it, Nick?' you said.

'Yeah,' I said. 'It's wicked. Congratulations. But I have to sleep. You understand me? I really have to sleep.'

'I get it, Nick. I completely get it. But see you later, okay? Maybe we can celebrate? Doubles at Chicken Cottage?'

Silence.

'Okay, Nick, I'm outta here. Later.'

You turned around, picked up the keys from the shelf and walked out.

You forgot to lock the front door. The sliding door was left half open. And the hall lamp burned like a sun out there, eating through my eyelids.

42

Since that day at Barista, when we drank hot chocolate and you read Malcolm X's autobiography, something has happened to you. I didn't notice at first. The change has been gradual. But you're turning into someone else. Someone who reads, thinks, grows.

Several signs point to this.

A moment ago you sent a video clip from the classroom to my telephone. Your grinning face filled the screen, and when I pressed the play button, a jarring sound cut into me.

'Do you get what I'm talking about now, Nick? This is how it is every day!'

You turned the camera around and panned across the classroom. It looked as if there was a riot going on. The desks had been turned upside down, a couple of pupils were lying on the floor, wrestling, while others stood on the windowsill by the wide-open window, yelling out into the playground. Chairs lay strewn all over the place. Just a few obedient kids sat at their desks, looking straight ahead. By the teacher's desk, his face partially hidden behind a book, sat the teacher, who was reading out loud. When once more you made a sweep of the camera a chair was flung through the air. *Whack*, it said, as it disappeared out of frame.

The improvement was clear: you weren't participating, you were filming from the bench where you now sat, by the wall at the front of the classroom. In eight months you'd raised your grades in all subjects except two. You'd achieved a grade A in a history test, and the teacher had written in the margin: *This is good, Elijah! And great that you've started debating with us – fantastic!*

What? When did all this happen?

After that visit to the cafe, you let the Malcolm X book lie for a week. You kept it within reach. So that it would entice you, maybe attract your attention. Soon you picked it up again and read a page. Then another. Until you had ploughed through half of it.

You were consumed by it. Keeping me informed on a running basis: 'Now I'm on page 198, Nick!' – 'I'm on page 260!'

You were named after Malcolm X's mentor, Elijah Muhammad, and you can identify with Malcolm's story. You've been inspired by what I've told you about it. But more important than the obvious pull of the subject is the fact that you have become a person who reads books. Literature has become accessible to you.

Your context is making a difference. You have been living with me for over a year. Every day you see me reading a book. It's not unusual for me to be talking in a worked-up tone of voice about books and politics with my friends. I'm frustrated but involved. It affects you. In the evenings you often ask about what I'm reading, and you ask me to read it out to you. It's become a way of spending time together without breaking up my routines. I no longer withdraw from you like I used to. Instead I stay there, sitting on the couch with you. I read out loud to you every night of the week now. At first it made no difference what book I had in my hand, and you quickly fell asleep. But then you became pickier. You wrapped the plaid around you, got yourself comfortable.

You said: 'Nick, will you read the yellow book instead? It's better.' Or: 'Nick, that one's boring, she's all over the place, get another one.'

The books varied, we switched between genres. But soon, for reasons beyond understanding, you fell for Karl Ove Knausgård's *My Struggle*. Exactly what appealed to you about it is difficult to say. The text is monotonous and lacks action, yet it's also beautiful and intimate in more senses than one. I told you that until quite recently, Knausgård had been living further down our street, and that almost the entire series had been written in the family's flat just by Triangel-torget in Malmö. You could hardly believe it.

'For real?' you said.

'For real. Also, Knausgård wrote about the street just outside; he described it in detail. And he made the same observation as we have. Listen here: "the higher up the street one came, the cheaper and more dubious the shops became. The same went for the people that shuffled about there." The people that shuffled about there, that live there – that's us!'

You were all agape. 'Read more, Nick! Read more!'

'Okay,' I said. 'Listen to this, see if you recognize where you are.'

I read a passage in which Knausgård describes the retailers, including the sex shop TABOO opposite the Greek joint, which you always glance at when you think I'm not looking. You sat bolt upright in the sofa.

'But that's here, bro!' you said. 'It's down below, we could go down and have a look at it right now.'

It was a huge moment. Even, perhaps, the greatest of all literary experiences. The book had moved into your life. You had moved into the book. And it got even better.

'You want to know something even more wicked?' You nodded. 'It's even possible – or, I mean, it's actually quite likely – that we're the people he's writing about. He mentions running into "immigrant boys", who "walk so damned slow it's as if they own the pavement" and teenage boys coming towards him: "Black, back-combed hair, black leather jackets, black trousers, and at least one of them has Puma shoes with the logo on the toe, which I've always thought looks so stupid. Gold chains around their necks, slightly unsteady, clumsy arm movements . . ."'

You stood up on the sofa and laughed uproariously into the air. 'So sick!' you wailed. 'That could be us!'

'Yeah, maybe,' I said. 'Even that crazy unpredictable white-haired lady who makes you so nervous is in it. You know, the one who drags herself down Södra Förstadsgatan and spits out curses and gives people the evil eye. She's in the book!'

These days we read Karl Ove Knausgård every night.

Or K-O as you like to call him. 'K-O' in English – *Kay Oh*.
You can't get enough of him.

As a way of developing your interest in language and books
and social and political issues, we have started discussing hip
hop. More specifically we discuss – and dissect – the lyrics
of the rappers, and what they're trying to say. It's opened up
a whole new way for you to listen to your idols.

'It's so fucked up, what he's really saying there,' you might
comment. 'He's such a sexist, Lil Wayne, plus he only talks
about money.' Or: 'Shit, Nas is so deep, like a prophet, man.'

And so the pieces fall into place: school becomes relevant
for you. My work acquires a deeper significance. Your own
situation can be expressed and understood in a political sense.

One evening, with your toothbrush in your mouth, you
called out from the bathroom: 'Class, Nick? What's really
meant by that?'

You try to decipher the concepts. You make a note of
them in your mobile phone and then you ask about them.
Class, sexism, power structure, human rights, norms . . .

We sat on the bed. I got out a notepad and sketched
pyramids and circles, sad and happy faces.

Class.

'Mmm,' you said. 'I think I get it. But that working-class
thing doesn't make sense. Everyone works, right? And if you
don't work, then you're unemployed.'

43

Yesterday you had breakfast and slipped off to school before I'd woken up. But when I stepped out of the shower, at about half past nine, you were back again. 'What are you doing here?' I asked. And then I pulled a joke: 'Did someone demolish the school?'

'No,' you said. 'But they found weapons on the roof. All classes are cancelled.'

'What?'

'Yeah, that's all they would tell us. They don't want to say anything else.'

We headed into the living room and turned on the computer to check the news. Malmö police were just holding a press conference. All the big media outlets were writing about the weapons find and publishing photos and video of your school: police with stern faces gathered in the playground, patrol cars parked outside the classrooms, and a plain-clothes police officer carrying a guitar case in front of curious by-standers outside the cordon.

The weapons had been found on the school roof the day

before. You'd been in the classroom, in the middle of a mathematics lesson, unaware that a construction worker above your head was opening a guitar case, in which there was an elk-hunting rifle equipped with telescopic sights, also a shotgun, and masses of ammunition.

The construction workers contacted the police. But the school authorities were only notified about the find in the afternoon. The school wasn't evacuated.

The event had brought up the subject of school shootings in Sweden. Headmasters, politicians and police all make statements on the importance of schools preparing for a mass shooting and sharpening up their routines.

The situation in the world, in a snapshot: you are expected to study, to plan for your future, and drill for the possibility of your own massacre.

At first I was dismissive of the news item. Of course, it's not unthinkable that your school, which has been characterized by violence and social instability, could be a setting for a shooting. But in this case, it would surely be some form of revenge against a specific person, not a lone lunatic firing indiscriminately. Or?

I leaned on statistics, found various sources on the net. How many Swedish schools have been subjected to mass shootings in the last decades? Zero. How many of the schools where mass shootings have occurred – irrespective of in what country – have been located in impoverished, immigration-background city areas? Hardly any. The risk of your school and you being caught up in such a thing, in other words, are minute. It calmed me to think like this. But then, when I thought through what little information I had on hand, my heart started beating.

Today is Saturday. The weapons were found on Thursday. On Friday the school was closed. On Monday it will open again as usual. The police are not ruling out that the weapons were going to be used against the children in a planned attack. If this is the case, then there's a high likelihood that the perpetrator is merely biding his time, waiting for a new occasion to come back and fulfil his plan. Right?

No, apparently not. Not according to the police and the school management.

The only measures that have been taken are that they have brought in *a team of counsellors for anxious students*, as well as a couple of security people who will be plodding about in the school grounds. Their joint assessment is: there is no perceived threat.

Which worries me. On what basis, for what reasons, is this not being taken more seriously? Surely one only has to use one's imagination. Consider the types of weapons that were found, and that the perpetrator has still not been caught, and that we know nothing about this person or their motive.

I grow conspiratorial.

If the arms cache had been found in a school on the other side of town, and the children there were potential targets for a school shooting, wouldn't the world have stopped? Wouldn't the parents have marched out to demand changes in the law?

Would not the school grounds have been filled with riot police? Would there not have been police helicopters hovering over the school's rooftops, and marksmen in position?

When six days have gone by since the weapons were found, there are no more security guards in evidence. No one mentions the event, and the newspapers have stopped writing about it. I don't know what I should be doing. I can't get it out of my head.

I fantasize about getting some news of a school shooting in Malmö. I think it must have been a case of someone drawn into a conflict, some gang shit; the kids that witnessed the shooting are traumatized, someone is dead. Then, I read it's not a normal shooting but a mass shooting, a lone perpetrator who's sprayed bullets wildly in all directions. I remain cool, I stay collected. I think to myself: this will change our perception of the teaching and learning environment, the role of teachers, the well-being of students, safety. Then I imagine that it's in Fosie. That's nothing to do with me, I think, I don't think I know any kids there, do I? In fact, yes. Your school is in Fosie. Although, it's just one of ten in that part of town. What are the odds of this having happened at your school? My pulse picks up. I click onto *Sydsvenskan*'s online edition.

BREAKING NEWS: Shooting at school in South-East Malmö. Many dead and wounded. Hundreds of shots fired. Suspected gunman shot dead by police.

Then I read that it's about your school. I feel giddy, I grip onto the tabletop to stop myself losing my balance. I turn around, I support myself with my hands against the wall, and teeter into the hall. I call your telephone. The signals go through, but you don't answer. I step into my shoes; put on my jacket and hurry down the stairwell. Ice-cold air buffets against my face as I pedal off at top speed. I call you again; I clamp the telephone against my ear as I pedal. No answer. By Södervärn, the ambulances are swishing past. The roads are lit up with spinning blue lights. Everything is at top volume. I pick up my mobile phone from my jacket pocket, reading as I steer with an unsteady hand.

Twenty-two confirmed dead, even more injured. The perpetrator was apparently wearing black and a baclava. The shooting began from the roof. Thereafter, the perpetrator made his way into the school building. The emergency services have taken multiple calls. Yelling voices and the sound of an echoing pistol clattering in the background, crying voices fleeing the scene.

Lactic acid streams through my legs. The taste of blood fills my mouth. Outside the school there's mayhem. People are hugging and weeping. Police all along the pavements. Cordon tape and broadcasting vans around the school perimeter. I jump off my bicycle while it's still moving and run up to the fence, standing on my tiptoes. In the playground I see emergency services staff and police, some of them squatting, others talking into their telephones, and everywhere bodies with sheets thrown over them. I lose contact with my thoughts and feelings. I've experienced it before, this feeling of hovering outside of myself. I make it over the fence and pick up speed, but I only have time to run a few metres before I'm bundled over and lying on the ground. That's when I see it. Over by the basketball court. Two bodies under yellow sheets. Under one of them, fluttering slightly in the wind, I can see it sticking out, my purple-orange scarf.

44

You couldn't wake up. Like a beached whale you lay sleeping, hour after hour, without reacting to any sound.

Finally I prodded the tip of your nose. 'Hello-o,' I said. 'Time to get up, half the day has gone.'

The beached whale gradually started looking like a knocked-out boxer. Your head was spinning and you smelled bad. Slowly you sat up on the edge of the camp bed, peering at me while the room spun into position.

You didn't only smell bad. You stank of genitalia.

'Shit,' you mumbled. 'How long have I been sleeping?'

'It's one thirty,' I said. 'You've missed both breakfast and lunch and I already went to work out. What happened yesterday?'

When I went to bed at about two in the morning you still weren't home. I sent you a text message and you answered, **Coming soon, busy here.**

A laugh flew out of you, and at once you were wide awake. Then your facial colour shifted to red, and you averted your eyes.

'What?' I said.

'You know what,' you said, laughing out loud. 'I did it, Nick. I fucking did it.' You looked at me and grew serious. 'Are you getting me, Nick? I did it!'

You'd lost your virginity. Until the early hours of the morning you were with a girl called Malin. She's much older than you, almost a grown-up. Or rather, she is a grown-up. She's twenty. You were together in the evening, you told me. And you felt something, felt as if she was making moves on you, as if she was flirting with you, trying to make you feel horny. It had been unexpected, you admitted. You'd had a sort of sibling relationship until then. But she wanted sex. Mainly for your sake, she implied to you. 'I can take your virginity if you like,' she said. An offer to which you, after thinking it over for zero seconds, had given a nod of agreement. But not without getting a tad insecure about it. It sounded too good to be true. It was wrong, at the same time as it was right. Because you were like siblings, you said. Like friends, or maybe a little more.

Malin had guided you through the process. Obediently you'd done as she said, and then you'd come, without using a condom. It was done and dusted quite quickly, as I understood it, and only after you parted ways and you cycled home, grinning from ear to ear, did you fully understand what you had done.

'Did you use a condom?' was the first thing I asked.

Again, I saw a flush on your face. 'No,' you sighed. But you had no regret; there was a smile hovering on your lips.

'Are you angry, Nick?' you said after a while. 'Do you think it was dumb of me?'

'Well,' I said. 'Your personal life is your own concern. But I don't get how you're going to combine having a little kid in Sweden with playing professionally in the US. It wouldn't be totally uncomplicated, as you can probably understand. Because if you do get into university, this means four years without an income. And Malin has her job here, right, so the kid would have to stay in Sweden. The alternative for you, then, would be to drop out of school, take a shit job, rustle up some cash, and support your family. Because you'd have to be a dad who's there and taking responsibility; anything else would be the total opposite of what you've told me. So all you can do then is to stay in Malmö and put your plans for the US on the shelf. No secondary school, no university. Later, after a year or so, with a contract that's good enough, and assuming Malin goes along with it, you might be able to live on your pay as a pro and move to Europe with your kid. But, like I say, that's years ahead. And it's far from certain that Malin will even want to be with you. Or I suppose it's unthinkable, actually. She's a grown woman. You're a child. And a child can't really bring up a baby.'

Your face had turned white as a sheet. 'Oh, come on . . .' you stammered. 'Don't say that, Nick. I wasn't going at it for very long. I came real quick.'

'Came real quick?' I said. 'Do you know that you only need one sperm to fertilize an egg? There are hundreds of millions of them in every ejaculation. Also, sperm can live inside the woman for days and wait for the egg. Do you understand how serious this is? Quite apart from that, it can't be ruled out that you've caught a venereal disease. It can't be much fun having blood-filled blisters on the head of your penis or to feel your dick burning when you take a piss. Not to mention the venereal diseases that could kill you, such as AIDS. All this because you don't listen to me. Never listen to me. We've talked about it a thousand times. And still you do the complete opposite of what I say.'

I got up from the couch and went into the kitchen. Not a sound came from the living room. I went into the hall, put on my shoes and jacket. I asked if you wanted to come out with me, but you stayed silent.

'Come on,' I said. 'We can talk about it on the way. It'll probably be fine.'

An aura of anguish hung over you. With a wilted neck and cement blocks on your feet, you shuffled along. We strolled aimlessly down Södra Förstadsgatan.

'Knausgård,' I said, pointing at an entrance. 'Just imagine, he lived there and wrote his books up there.' I nodded at the balcony on the top floor. 'That's where he used to sit,' I said, 'looking out over Malmö, writing about his city, which is also your city. He wrote about this square. Wrote about that Asian restaurant. Wrote about the hotel. That's just sick. It is, though, isn't it?'

You weren't listening. Nothing was getting through.

'But,' I said, 'what will happen now with that girl you said you were crushing on? What was her name again? Jessica?'

You looked at me for the first time since we walked out of the apartment. You'd met Jessica during the county team selection process. She lived in Stockholm.

'You were in love with each other, I thought?'

Once more a shadow fell over your face.

'Yeah, Nick,' you said, with a sigh.

'Things are not adding up for me, brother?' I said. 'You're

in love with Jessica, you've planned to meet up. But you choose to go to bed with another girl. What's your thinking there?'

We turned into the pedestrian street and continued towards Gustav Adolfs Plaza. You hadn't eaten anything after waking up, you had dark rings under your eyes and you looked almost ill. I thought about lightening up the atmosphere, but you suddenly stopped and looked much less weighed down.

'You know, Nick,' you said. 'I know how I can do this. I keep talking to Jessica, I tell her I can come up to Stockholm, but I push it. I tell her she can come to Malmö if she wants, but it'll have to be later once we've fixed up some cash and all that. Then I wait and check out the lie of the land with Malin. If she's not . . . well . . . you know . . . If everything works out, I'll see Jessica afterwards. And then I don't have to say anything to her. At the same time it's like I'm punishing myself, because I want to see Jessica so badly. But I'm not letting myself do it. Do you get what I mean? What do you think of that?'

45

Your first gig with the national team was a fiasco. Even before I met you at the train station on your arrival there from Copenhagen, I knew how you were feeling.

I'd seen the games live on YouTube. It was looking surprisingly good. Not the team's performance – as a team you were lamentable. But you sometimes performed beyond expectation and were the highest scorer in the Swedish team.

The Germans beat you by eighty points. I could hardly watch. You beat the Danes. Serbia was too good for you. Whatever the result, I felt proud seeing you in the blue and yellow jersey, and the quality of your performance.

Your downbeat mood when you came back had to do with your coach.

The sound of raucous voices, wolf-whistles, shoes squeaking against the floor, the applause and horns of the audience, meant that I didn't notice it at first. But then the coach's voice cut through the buzz. *What the hell's he yelling for?* I thought, and tried to understand what was happening. It's not unusual for inexperienced coaches to be as physically active on the court as the players, running up and down the sidelines, gesturing. But then I understood that it was you he was scolding.

'For Christ's sake, Elijah!' he yelled so loudly that it echoed in the hall. 'Pass the ball! You're not Michael Jordan! Elijah, what the hell are you doing? Stick to what we said!'

He called you over and gave you a dressing-down in front of everyone watching: your teammates, the audience, the rest of us at home by our computers.

When you feel that you are being unfairly treated, I can see it immediately in your body language. And for every game your shoulders came down more and more. The criticism was not only demeaning, it was also incoherent and difficult to transform into anything constructive.

When you came walking up the escalator at Triangeln station I could see that you were broken. I stood by the ticket machines looking down at you. You'd slung your bag over your shoulder, your hair was a mess, and your eyes were red as if you'd just been crying.

I hugged you, took your bag.

'Did you see, Nick?' you asked, without having to say anything more.

'I saw,' I said. 'You should be proud of yourself, there's nothing to get sad about here. You did really well.'

But you were sad, and disappointed. Just for once this wasn't directed at yourself, but at the coach, because the rumours had been proved right.

Throughout your childhood you'd been told that Swedish sport, and specifically Swedish basketball, was not for you. The older *blattes* had fed you on a diet of scepticism and conspiracy theories about your sport, your club, your coaches. You'd been told there was nothing to be gained here, it made no difference if you were good, if you had talent and stood out from the mass. If you were a *blatte*, the Swedie boys and the Swedish Sports Confederation would find a way of grinding you down, pushing you out, make you doubt yourself and your abilities, and get you out prematurely.

'Just check out what happens!' they said. 'We dominate in our early years, we're the biggest talent, we get things done. But the Swedie boys are holding out in the shadows, watching everything and forging their plans. Then, on the way to the top, we fall by the wayside one after another, until the elite team looks like a gang of blond and blue-eyed Scandinavian caricatures. We don't have a chance. And the quicker you get this, Elijah, and leave Sweden, the better.'

I am one of these bitter, conspiracy-prone *blattes* myself. Although, I did admittedly have the chance to keep playing. At the age of twenty-three I had professional contracts offered by several Swedish league clubs and offers of salaries and paid-for accommodation. Three years earlier I'd been offered full scholarships from two universities in the USA.

But I was afraid. I didn't dare go for it. I remember the conversation with Anderson University and that worked-up booming voice: 'We want you, Nicolas!' and then I remember how I almost burst out laughing because it just sounded so damn ludicrous. *Do you really think I'm going to give up what little security I have here, in my impoverished loneliness, so that I can head off to a new country and pulverize the only dream I ever had? You must be crazy!*

I didn't say that. I thanked them for their generosity, said I'd think about it, felt a certain pride about the Americans seeing a value in me, which lifted me off the ground. At the same time, I think I may have understood how far I was from being able to spread my wings, which was discouraging, and I never called them back.

I live on unrealized credentials in basketball. And if I have the opportunity to brag in front of my friends, colleagues or a stranger at some party, I tell them I could have become a pro, the offers were pouring in, and I still have the points scoring record in Division 1.

'You see, I was kind of a phenomenon, not even five foot ten, quick as hell and not worried about the big fuckers, but I just couldn't take playing any more, you know. There's more to life than throwing a ball around. Sport has become so commercialized, so elitist in its essence, so excluding and racist and homophobic that I decided to work with children instead.'

'Wow,' they say. 'That was big of you and well thought through.'

'Yes,' I say. 'It certainly was. I'm big and well thought through, the whole lot of me.'

I'm bitter because the Swedish Sports Confederation is rotten to the core. If you belong to the lower classes, if you're a woman, *blatte*, trans or you have physical disabilities, then the motto of the Swedish Sports Confederation, 'a sporting movement for all', is like being gobbed at in the face.

But my opinions and my bitterness wouldn't help you one little bit. If I shared them with you, the way all those averagely talented *blattes* have done throughout your childhood, you would start looking for reasons why things are not going your way, find people to blame for your shortcomings, and in this way ruin the possibility of living up to your potential and realizing your dreams. Then turn into a bitter, conspiratorial *blatte* yourself.

But you do feel it in your body, you know it's happening. Your place in sport, in basketball, is conditional. There are powers on every level that will work against you.

46

It's all happened very fast. A few weeks after the tour in Germany, your older brother called from San Diego where he lives. An American basketball agent based in Europe has been watching your games, been impressed by your play. He tried to find the contact details of your guardian, finally turning to your older brother with grandiose plans for your future.

Your brother told you that next year, when you turned sixteen, you could get a grant which would cover all the costs of playing, living and studying in the USA. The agent had said it was possible that he'd land a deal.

It was an unbelievable thought. Totally absurd. To the extent that, when you recapped your conversation, I grew irritated about your brother giving you false expectations.

I'd never heard of a player – whether talented or not – who'd been offered such an opportunity at such an early stage. For outstandingly talented players – which are few in Sweden – the chance only comes up at university. I tried to lower your expectations.

'It's probably going to be tough,' I said, 'not to say impossible. Don't get your hopes up too much.'

But you didn't listen to me. When you'd finished your call

you stood in the living room with the telephone in your hand, yelling: 'It can't be true, Nick, it just can't be true!'

The telephone was red hot for the next few weeks. The agent was already in contact with schools on the American east coast, in the state of Maryland. 'Be prepared to go if they want you to visit,' was your older brother's recommendation. *With what money?* I thought.

The obstacles were towering up in front of me. First, the unlikelihood of it actually happening. Then the endless questions: would the ossified school bureaucracy in Sweden allow such a sudden move? Would we be able to produce all the documents – student visa, accredited grades, and so on – in time? Would your mother, your legal guardian, who needed to take care of the conversations with the school and the authorities, have any objections? Not to mention the expenses that the school would not be paying – pocket money, clothes, air travel back and forth. Who would be covering it?

My scepticism was based also on my own impressions of American sports agents. No professionals that I have ever run into are more well-spoken, intrusive, artificial and rapacious. There are few people that you could have less of a reason to trust. And yet, you need an agent with insight and contacts in order to make the decisions in all things that touch upon your future career in basketball.

I stayed out of the conversations. Didn't want to be involved in a high-altitude plan that would fall to pieces. And further, my knowledge of the necessary procedures was limited, to say the least.

And also: I didn't want you to go.

47

Two thirty in the morning. I was standing in the kitchen, folding your clean laundry, when a text message came in from my colleague, Mathi:

There's a fucking riot going on outside my entrance. People being attacked with glass bottles. They're running and yelling and lying injured on the ground. Real chaos!

I answered:

Keep me updated, please. And don't even think about going out there and getting drawn into that shit.

Moments later he wrote again:

One injured man came back and lay down on the ground. Still chaos. Serious Crime Unit, horses, cars . . . the ambulance is here. It took those bastards 15 minutes to show up. But it should be all right. They've carried the guy into the ambulance. If it had been serious, they would have driven off with their sirens on.

The following morning I had four missed calls and a text message.

Mathi wrote:

Attempted murder of 4 people. One of them is Showan. He's in the hospital. I'm going over there now. Call you later.

After a couple of hours Mathi got in touch again and confirmed that Showan's condition was critical and that a demonstration was being organized in the square in Möllan that same night.

When you woke up, I told you that a friend had been assaulted and that he might die, and that we were taking part in a demonstration.

'It's not going to work,' you said tersely. Then reached for the flat energy drink you'd left by the bed, slurped it, and pointed at your bandaged foot.

You'd twisted your ankle in yesterday's practice. When you got back, limping, your ankle was horribly swollen and there was a dark purple streak running along the edge of the sole. The foot had been badly bandaged. The person helping you hadn't known how to apply a pressure bandage, the tape was loose, and further you hadn't put your foot up. This mistake increased the risk of an extended rehabilitation period and making it even more painful. I told you this. I said it could cause you long, possibly even irreparable problems – in principle, almost like being handicapped.

'Floppy ankles is the worst thing that can happen to a basketball player,' I said. 'You understand that you guys fucked it up, right? It's crucial when you twist your ankle, you have to act quick as a flash and be resolute about it and shut down the blood flow to the foot. But you know that, everyone knows that.'

I said it like that because I wanted you to suffer. I wanted you to feel it in your heart and soul. And you did. You were close to tears.

It hurt so badly when you put any weight on the foot that I fetched down my crutches from the attic. You stood on one leg in the living room, gripping the handles, taking a couple of trial steps. You swayed, couldn't quite get the hang of the movements. And muttered like an old man when I said we should go.

We sat in Chicken Cottage and looked out over the square, which was gradually filling with people. The atmosphere was eerie. People were downcast, crying, half of them pale as ghosts. And that's when I allowed myself to feel, or really understand, what had happened. Showan was fighting for his life . . .

Mathi called, in a worked-up state. He told me what I'd already found out. Several of the victims had been stabbed, and Showan's skull had been stamped on, against the edge of a pavement stone. The assailants were Nazis. The police later confirmed this. The newspapers wrote that it had been a dust-up between people on the fringes of the right and left.

A dust-up.

The thought of it is ridiculous. Showan wouldn't be able to do any harm to anyone with his bare fists. He weighs fifty kilos. Mathi says that on the street beneath his flat there's still shattered glass, and the blood from Showan's broken skull has painted the edge of the pavement red.

You met Showan last summer at the House of the People in Sofielund. He held forth with a monologue on the working class, and how his loyalty to it is unshakeable. You didn't know that we had gathered here for Showan and his friends. You didn't ask. You were irritatingly self-absorbed; you gnawed a chicken bone and fiddled listlessly with your phone.

'Let's get out of here,' I said, and pulled down your hood. You stuffed your mouth full of French fries and we joined the crowd outside.

48

Showan's skull has been crushed. Also, the Nazis have stabbed him in the back with a knife.

'Showan will either die,' says Mathi, 'or he'll be a vegetable.'

The day began with this information.

You sat hunched over your cereal, slurping and whining. You couldn't understand that you had to go to school. You said that no normal person would go to school if their legs wouldn't bear their weight. That's not how you said it, you don't express yourself that way. But you limped into the hall, grunted, threw your rucksack over your shoulder, and slammed the door.

I feel deeply unhappy. It often happens nowadays that I'm overcome with sorrow.

I miss my mother.

Sometimes, voluntarily or involuntarily, it's hard to know which, I gaze out into the all-enveloping darkness; Mum will never exist again. She's gone. I have to live without her. During all these years, I've repressed it. I just sense these little pinpricks of panic, which could easily devour everything inside with a despair so deep that I wouldn't have the strength to go on living.

*   *   *

A couple of years ago I found out that Anja, the girl who was with us during my growing up, had had a son. She was young when she got pregnant, just eighteen or nineteen. I've often wondered what became of her, how she is, and what sort of parent she is. We've run into each other on a couple of occasions over the years, and every time she's said the same thing. That Mum was an angel in her life. That she was the best thing that happened to her in her childhood. That she misses her so much that it hurts. A few times she's broken down in tears in my arms. Her affection answers another thing I've repeatedly mused on. How did she view the rupture with Mum? Did she have a sense that Mum had let her down or abandoned her? What really happened to Anja when she stopped coming by to see us? Mum would have been ecstatic if she'd learned that Anja was a parent. It would have been a guarantee that if she failed to live happily, then at least she wouldn't be alone. As Mum saw it, I like to think, a child was a more important and reliable companion than a spouse. With her son, Anja would be able to grow old and always have someone by her side. Possibly Mum might also have considered this son as her grandchild. This thought is immeasurably sad.

I want to be a parent. A father. Have my own children. Find some meaning.

It feels stupid to long for people who do not exist.

Stupid to think that Mum will never get to meet them.

Nina Elisabet Lunabba's grandchildren.

I've never thought that way before. It can't be countenanced. The pain of it. An interrupted continuum. An eternity, which will never exist.

Earlier today I walked past the square in Möllan without being on my way to anywhere in particular. The market stallholders seemed in low spirits. No sign of any hipsters anywhere. Just the cold sun, and the wind tearing at the crowns of the trees.

I sat on one of the benches outside the hamburger joint. And even though I was wearing sunglasses and a baseball cap, Josef caught sight of me from a distance. He came up to say hello. As usual, he was cheerful and shy.

'How are things, brother? All good?' I asked.

'Yes, king,' he said with a wry smile.

'And the family?'

'It's all good, brother. How are things with you, Nick?'

'Okay. Lots of work, as usual.'

Josef told me that he wanted to get back into basketball. That he missed practice and the team. Missed us. Despite not training for the regional camp, not having played a game in over two months, he was picked for the national youth team.

He held out his hand, I shook it, stood up and hugged him. He was already half a head taller than me. His face was so covered in spots that there were little craters of pus and blood erupting all over it. He was dishevelled, which contrasted with the strong scent of aftershave and the outfit he was wearing – branded clothes from head to toe. His bulletproof vest was as hard as a suit of armour under his jacket.

49

In the end, Mark, the agent, called. He presented three schools that had expressed an interest in offering you a place, with a full scholarship. But first they wanted to meet you and get copies of your school reports. We had to quickly have them translated into English. Next up came the task that might just be impossible – finding a host family for you, which was Mark's job.

Mark explained how the schools looked at things, and how the logistics and practicalities might play out. He said that the students in one of the schools lived in a student residence, which meant that, there, the problem was solved.

'On the other hand,' said Mark, in a more serious tone of voice, 'living and studying there would mean that Elijah had to stay on campus.'

'Right,' I said, 'but surely that's no problem?'

'Well,' said Mark, 'that would depend on how disciplined he is. The students in school residence can only leave campus for a couple of hours once every week. And the boys can't have any female visitors in their rooms. There's a strict code of conduct, and if the students break the rules or fail their tests or come late to classes, there's a high risk that they'll be kicked out. But if you feel that you can live up to all that, Elijah, then this school might be the best one for you.'

'Of course he'll manage it,' I said, with a wink at you. 'No problem at all.'

'The other two schools require us to find host families,' Mark went on, 'which is easier said than done. But now I'm putting the cart before the horse. The first thing you need to do is have the school report cards translated, then go over for a visit.'

'Okay,' I said, 'we'll get that sorted. When do the schools want us to come?'

'When can you come?'

50

As if out of nowhere, you and I find ourselves sitting on a plane ten thousand metres above the Atlantic Ocean.

We land in New York, which for the last few weeks has been hit by snowstorms. It's unlike the weather I've experienced in northern Sweden in winter. There, the air is fresh, the view is clear, the landscape soft and inviting. To breathe in New York is to inhale liquid ice into one's lungs. The temperature sinks to minus ten during the nights, there's a driving horizontal wind in the avenues, and one has to walk leaning forward to avoid getting snow crystals in one's eyes. Unlike the Swedish winter with its white, round contours, the New York winter is hard, sharp-edged and, despite all the artificial light, thoroughly dark. Everywhere stone, glass and metal. The pavements are like tunnels of hard-packed ice. Stiletto-sharp, up to half-metre-long icicles hanging from drainpipes and street lights. Tall buildings disappearing into nothingness when one peers up at the grey and black sky. The trains and planes are cancelled and the schools are closed. The authorities have issued warnings about venturing out of doors, and so the city centre is unnervingly depopulated.

The warnings do not apply to us. We are only here for

three days before travelling to Maryland to meet with Mark and visit three schools. We try to take in the fact that we are here. We have exchanged our drab existence in Möllan to traipse about here in the USA. It's inexplicably huge. In case it all screws up we can at least say that we got a lot out of our visit to New York.

We both sense that our time together is coming to an end. If you're offered a full scholarship, the next few months will be a slow break-up, which, at the end of the summer, will culminate in a last farewell. During breakfast, while you chomped down the biggest baguette I had ever seen and drank fizzy drinks from a litre-sized cup, you described how you imagined your future would be. First three years at secondary school, thereafter three or four years at university, followed by a long professional career in the NBA.

I corrected: 'Or Europe, if no NBA.'

'No, Nick!' you roared. 'No, no, no! You think I can't get into the NBA or what? Don't you think I've got it in me?'

The bar is placed very high, but if your goals were laughable a year ago, they're not quite as unrealistic now. Nonetheless I feel duty-bound to inform you of the dangers of putting all your eggs in one basket.

'You need to find a balance, Elijah,' I say. 'There have to be other things than basketball that add value to your life, other possible scenarios for the future.'

'What do you mean, Nick?' you say wearily, with an irritated glare at me. 'Obviously I'm going to fucking go for it. We always have done. We just fucking go.'

*　　*　　*

Our approaching parting has lodged in your body, and you deal with the discomfort by pushing me away. In a matter of just a few days, you have become unpleasant and defiant. As we walk around the icy smooth streets of New York, you still with a slight limp on your bad foot, and I ask you to hold the ball, which you insist on dribbling, you snort at me: 'I can do what I want!' Only to stumble in the next second and watch the ball rolling off into the traffic or under a snow-covered bus or car. Then, you become like a three-year-old, and you whimper pleadingly: 'Niiick . . . Please, can you get it?'

In the morning we went by Madison Square Garden and the Empire State Building, had lunch and hung out in Times Square, before moving on to Harlem. We searched in vain there for the outlet boutiques, tracked down the Audubon Ballroom where Malcolm X was murdered, stood about outside, unsure of whether we'd found the right place, and took lots of photos just to be on the safe side.

You really wanted to get a haircut in a proper barber shop, and after a certain amount of dithering we found a little salon half hidden under a floppy, stained awning. The owner, an elderly retired captain in the American navy who'd covered the walls of the salon with black-and-white framed photos of soldiers and enormous warships, welcomed us. During the forty-five minutes that he spent cutting your hair, not a single facial muscle was activated. He said nothing, and he mainly seemed disappointed that we happened to have found him in particular. Thereafter we strolled to Rucker Park, to visit the legendary basketball court where so many NBA stars had once played.

The park lay in a poor area with brick-red, thirty-storey residential blocks on one side and the Harlem River on the other. We walked along Frederick Douglass Boulevard, past West 155th Street, and had the park on our right-hand side. You talked about all the great players that had played at Rucker: Wilt Chamberlain, Kareem Abdul-Jabbar, Julius Erving, Kobe Bryant, Allen Iverson. And how people who wanted to catch a glimpse of their idols used to climb into the trees or up the street lights or onto the rooftops.

'Here it is,' I interrupted, and pointed at the sign. Holcombe Rucker Park.

'Shit,' you said and abruptly stopped. Held your breath. Looked through the fence, looked at me.

'Where?'

'There,' I said, and nodded at the vermilion green five-tiered stand, which could be seen indistinctly through the bare trees.

We opened the gate, and as soon as we reached the court, you plodded through the snow drifts and started taking shots at the basket. 'Take a photo of me, Nick,' you said. 'Take tons of photos! So we remember we were here!'

51

'You must be Nick,' said a voice from the forest of bodies that crowded the arrivals hall in the airport in Maryland. Then he stepped forward, Mark, and offered me his hand. 'Nice to meet you.'

'Nice to meet you too, Mark,' I said. 'Thank you so much for helping us out.'

'How you doing, buddy?' he said and turned to you.

You smiled so broadly that your eyes turned into slits. You put your limp hand in his and squeaked: 'Good.'

Mark was a pale greyish gentleman with thinning hair of an age somewhere between thirty and fifty. In the back seat of his dark blue city jeep, a child's chair was strapped in, meaning that he was clearly also the parent of a toddler. He opened the back door, pushed a couple of toys and a chewed-up drinking straw on the floor, told you to get in, and then opened the passenger door for me.

While we zigzagged between vehicles and barriers in the parking area, Mark told me about the schools we were visiting. The first one was called Episcopal High School and lay in the town of Alexandria south of Washington DC.

As Mark would have it, Episcopal was not only one of the most expensive boarding schools of the region but also one of the most prestigious. After that we'd squeeze in two 'reputable' private schools in two days: Bullis School in the town of Potomac and St Maria Goretti High School in Hagerstown, Maryland.

As we pulled onto the motorway, I thought about who he was, this Mark, and what his intentions were. He wasn't at all the sort of talkative and bragging American type that I'd been dreading, which made me feel both relieved and suspicious. I felt that his manner was artful, and that everything he said was carefully considered, because his foremost task in the next few days was to win our trust.

Mark, one assumed, had a fixed salary with a commission on the transfers he secured. His job was all about finding those nuggets of gold, and to convince management that they were worth putting time and resources into, while they waited for payback. In other words, you weren't worth shit yet, and you wouldn't earn Mark or the agency a penny until you signed your first professional contract, which in the best of worlds would happen in four to six years. While waiting for this, Mark's job would be all about avoidance of any talk of contracts and money, keeping on good terms with you, being available to give sage advice, and hoping that you didn't dump him for anyone else. As a rule, athletes trying to break into the elite are often narcissists, immature and superstitious, surrounding themselves with people who believe they know what's best for them. So, even though Mark and the agency merely saw you as a future investment, and even if they

---

turned their backs on you the second you were no longer considered a profitable bet, we should still be grateful that he chose you, an unknown fifteen-year-old from Sweden.

52

Episcopal High School was a dream. Mark had told us in advance about the strict rules and what happened to those who broke them. But as we were strolling across the campus, with students in school uniform swishing by, giggling, holding piles of books in their arms, some rap music thundered from an open window and the overall impression was something quite different. Coach Fitzpatrick, the trainer of the boys' team who met us outside the sports hall, exuded the same laid-back approach. He was about my own age, smiling as he spoke, and he had a warm, professional air about him.

'The young folk who play in the school's basketball team are high-school students, but we treat them as thoroughbred professionals here,' he announced proudly. 'They get their training clothes – yeah, even their underpants – washed, they have their own name on their booth in the changing rooms, and they have a buffet lunch.'

Coach Fitzpatrick stood with his hands on his hips, looking out over the basketball court's highly polished parquet floor with the school logo – a large E partitioned diagonally in white and wine red – painted across the central circle. He nodded at us and smiled: 'Neat, ain't it?' Yeah, we nodded back. It was so bloody neat. And when he later gave each of us an information folder and asked me to read the top line out loud, the atmosphere grew so lofty that we were ready to expire.

Our Mission: Guided by its founding principles of honor, academic distinction, spiritual growth, and community, Episcopal High School prepares young people with the intellectual and moral courage to pursue lives of ethical leadership and service as citizens of an increasingly connected world.

The morning after we headed off to Bullis School. After a two-hour car journey, we pulled into the school's parking area, where we were welcomed by the trainer, Coach Johnson. Like Coach Fitzpatrick, he was cheerful and relaxed. But when he greeted us, I felt I could see a fragment of insecurity in his gaze. He boasted about how qualified he was to coach 'the great Swede'. I could smell a rat. And sure enough, soon we found out that the school's basketball team had a low ranking and only played against the district's worst schools.

'It could be to your advantage, Elijah,' Coach Johnson said. 'You'll get a lot of space here and as a result you'll have the college recruiters' eyes on you.'

'That was a long shot,' Mark admitted as we had lunch in the school canteen. 'But if everything else fails, we still have Bullis as an alternative.'

In the car on the way from the school, Mark surprised us

with two VIP tickets to the big game that night: University of Maryland vs Wake Forest University.

'You're in the fourth row,' said Mark, 'to one side behind the home team's bench. If you're in the mood to go, I mean?' He winked at me.

'Of course we are!' you burst out, in Swedish.

Then you realized, and said: 'Thank you, Mark!'

'Don't thank me,' said Mark. 'It's the team management that's inviting us. But we might as well go over right away. There's often a jam outside the arena.'

The match was low-energy but the atmosphere was good. Only towards the end did the players come to life and the spectators jumped to their feet. Mark came bouncing down the stairs when the final signal went. 'Come on,' he said, and went down to the court. 'I want you to meet an old friend of mine.'

We hurried along behind him, went into the players' tunnel, through culvert-like corridors, upstairs, and through a large glass door into a gigantic office floor.

'These are the team headquarters,' I whispered to you, as if you didn't already know. 'This is where they sign the fat contracts.'

'Here's his office,' said Mark, knocking on a door.

It was opened by a big man with an imposing aura. He smiled and closed his enormous hand around mine. 'Welcome, gentlemen,' he said, introducing himself. 'I've heard so much about you, Elijah. Take a seat.'

The office walls were decorated with trophies and photographs of the Maryland University men's team. The large shelves were filled with files, books and photos of family members. The man was built like a heavyweight boxer, and his grey suit was loose-fitting and swung about like a tailcoat when he walked. We sat on a two-seater couch while Mark stayed in the doorway with his arms crossed. Our host sat down at a big marble table and started fingering a cigar.

'So what did you think of the game, my friend?' he said and looked at you.

You squeaked: 'Good.'

On his table were three takeaway boxes with *Mac-n-cheese* in red letters over the sealed plastic. 'I'm actually not allowed to give you anything. It would be seen as a bribe.' He chuckled. 'But, Mark, if you give them a box, I'll pretend I didn't notice.'

Mark did as the man said. I broke the plastic seal and stuck my plastic fork into the goo. You did the same, but you remained with the box in your lap. The man embodied my prejudices about Italian-Americans. He waved his hands around, swore, pulled his fingers through his wavy, black hair. He told us about the unrivalled training programme of the men's team, how the players here were treated like royalty, not least by the female students. He chortled. Mark winked at you. We were in a film. The man blurted out the names, unknown to me, of a lot of players from the university that had 'made it' and now 'made millions in the NBA and Europe'. I don't remember the man's exact position, but he was without a doubt a high-flier who could pull some strings if required.

Mark put his hand on your shoulder as we came out of the arena. 'They really want you to succeed, Elijah. They'll follow your development. If things go well, you have a sure spot on the team.'

The last stop on the USA trip was St Maria Goretti High School. You were already firmly decided that Episcopal was the school for you, and you seemed almost bothered by yet another visit. But then we walked into 'Goretti', which, unlike Episcopal's professional reception and exclusivity, felt almost familial. Here, it was the principal of the school, Miss Keenan-Bartholomew, who met us in the parking area. She was in a lively mood; she pinched your cheeks. We walked down the corridors, looked into classrooms where students in school uniforms sat immersed in their studies. We came to the staffroom and Ms Katrina came spinning out of the door. She was responsible for school admissions and, with this in mind, was certainly the most important person to impress. But Ms Katrina seemed impermeable to flattery. She was relaxed and natural. She hugged you as if you were already a part of the family.

After lunch you trained with the school's boys' team. You still had some pain in your foot, but you gritted your teeth and put in a good performance. The head coach, Rayfield, lavished praise on you. 'Young man, you're a great talent,' he said. 'Your style of play is very American, and you'd be a big asset to our team.'

What was going through your head as you sat there on the bench afterwards, wearing the Goretti jersey that Coach Rayfield had given you, wasn't easy to guess. Did it occur to you that this was too good to be true? If you were accepted, would you promise to follow the rules instead of performing your role as the *blatte* from Nydala? Would you swot and train hard and under no circumstances fuck up?

With clouds beneath your feet and the horizon reddened

by the sinking sun outside the little window, you slept peace-fully on the plane heading back to Sweden that same evening.

I sat in the adjoining seat and watched you. Amazed, as on so many other occasions, about your ability to sleep with total immersion.

I remembered your first night in my apartment. How afraid I'd been. My anxiety about what would happen to us, happen to me. You were so fragile and exposed. The decision to let you sleep over was irrevocable, and the future was frighteningly uncertain. And yet, in some strange way, there's even more at stake now than there was then.

At that time, your expectations had been so low that everything that happened to you, particularly having me so close to hand, was an upgrade of your previous situation. The chaotic present, so filled with obstacles and dangers, required your full attention. Dreams were a luxury you couldn't allow yourself, and therefore my task was simple and rewarding, even though it felt overwhelming in that moment: to give you a secure home and provide for your basic needs. With time, these factors have made you more secure, calmer and more empathic. They've made you a better basketball player, a good student, and facilitated this new situation, with the door open by a crack to the USA.

So here we are, then. Spring approaches. My feeling is it's going to be a long one, with an unbearable amount of waiting, and disappointments you'll take a long time to recover from. Your dreams, Elijah, will probably be crushed.

53

I can't allow myself any emotions. Neither anguish nor sorrow. Instead there's a kind of anticipation inside. It's horrible and it's out of place, but it's better than bottomless despair.

You call me from school and you say that the person who's blown himself up is Josef. He accidentally blew himself up when actually he was supposed to be blowing someone else up.

'Blow up what?' I say. Rebuffing you. 'What are you talking about?'

'I swear, Nick, it's him. It's Josef they're talking about.'

'You couldn't possibly know that,' I said. 'Is it Radi who's mouthing off? Radi just talks shit. No one knows for sure.'

'Yeah,' you insist. 'That's exactly what we know. Radi checked with David who knows it was planned, Josef was going to blow up the house. Blow up a man who lived in the house. But he blew up himself. It was him, Nick. Everyone's saying it.'

I sit at the computer in the kitchen. My mouth is dry. My body is numb. There's a heaviness and a stillness, while at the same time my heart is thumping. This moment is filled with meaning, a sense of destiny, as if everything in the whole world is concentrated into what's happening here and now. You and Radi have cycled from school to the place where the explosion took place. You're meeting Acke and Ibbe, who recently had contact with Josef. You're going to ferret about for information, ask around.

Obviously, I know it was Josef. I know without even knowing.

Rahim called ten minutes ago while I was fussing with you on the telephone. But I won't call back. Not yet. First, I'm going to find out what I can, top up my information sources, steel myself. I'm going to snoop about, surf around, scrutinize every lead, until there's no further doubt about it.

Late last night a bomb was planted outside the door of an apartment in a block in Sofielund, in which there lived several families. A number of newspapers have been there, publishing photos of the devastation and interviewing the residents. I read: *Teenager hospitalized with life-threatening injuries, after an explosion in which his own involvement is suspected.*

The details are grotesque. One resident says: 'The whole house shook. The young man who blew himself up was seriously hurt. The ambulance personnel were picking up body parts afterwards.'

Another resident says: 'Apparently, there was a youth in jeans and a hoodie calling for help after the detonation. Terrible screams, which quickly grew faint.' A police officer commenting on it has already drawn the conclusion that the young man, or child, in view of the fact that he's a minor, very likely was acting on behalf of someone else. The relevant person has previously been convicted of robbery and narcotics offences.'

A career criminal, living in that apartment, was believed to be the target of the attack. Also, the man's family was living there – his wife and three children. The boy used a military grade plastic explosive. According to police, the device was a so-called thermos bomb. But as the flat was equipped with a special security door, only the boy himself was injured by the explosion.

In a photograph I can see how the door of the flat has buckled inwards, how a crater has formed in the concrete floor, and how bomb shrapnel has sprayed in all directions, leaving bullet-like marks in the door and over the walls. Windows in the stairwell have been blown out. A couple of other apartments have had their doors destroyed and blown off their hinges. I see no blood. But one can easily imagine how a child's body has been flung backwards by the pressure wave of the detonation and torn to shreds by a burning swarm of metal and glass.

I don't find any other information. I update pages, I keep searching, but there's nothing else. I continue scrolling down through threads in Flashback. Hundreds of comments have been posted:

Wonderful! Instant karma! . . . Hope that Muslim piece of shit dies so society doesn't have to keep paying the bills for this mutilated bastard for the next 60 years . . . Not even Allah was with him this time, judging by the state of that hall . . . Talk about tasting your own medicine!

In the thread I find a link to more photographs from the crime scene: forensic technicians in full gear inside the stairwell, the ambulance crew in the midst of giving first aid, a body lifted onto a stretcher and into an ambulance.

The face in the images is pixellated, it's impossible to make out any details other than the boy's wavy black hair. The body is covered with a blanket and here and there one can see red patches of blood. In the description it's stated that the boy was taken to an A&E ward in Malmö, where he's being treated for life-threatening injuries. The last thing I read is that a police officer who was there at the scene doesn't believe the boy will pull through. 'I have a hard time believing it,' he repeats. 'I have a hard time believing it.' And on Flashback they're saying he's already dead. In the end I call Rahim. He says he thinks it's Josef. But he's not entirely certain.

54

For a couple of days we don't hear anything about the explosion. Nothing official about whether the boy is dead, the state of his injuries, or who he is.

You're as repetitious as a parrot: 'It's him, Nick. I'm telling you. Everyone knows. It's Josef.'

You're nervy and distracted. Since it happened you've been out till late in the evenings and you've resumed contact with your old gang. You say you're digging. 'We're digging, Nick. We're just digging for more information.' Earlier today while we were having lunch at the Greek's, you said you knew who'd assigned Josef, in other words the identity of the man who convinced him to plant the bomb, and I'm worried that it's him you're after. You ate without any appetite. You tore a piece of meat off the skewer but left the rest, one of your knees was juddering under the table, and your phone was constantly vibrating with incoming text messages. You left the restaurant before I'd finished my food.

You've been skipping practice. As soon as you wake up, or immediately after school, you want to head off. I'm having trouble gauging your mood. I'd like to be severe and make you stay at home with me. But this would risk having the opposite effect, of you not coming back at all.

Everything points to Josef. That we still don't know says a great deal about how isolated he has been, also from those closest to him. According to rumour, he was violent to his carers at the juvenile detention centre where he was living, and he assaulted others taken into care. This caused his transfer to another facility with a stricter regime, from which he did a bunk just before he planted the bomb.

You keep nagging me to come and see the house, say that I can only understand the devastation if I see it with my own eyes. There's a compulsive element there, you just don't give up.

Last night we cycled over there. We passed Sevedsplan and the big block of concrete covered in graffiti in the middle of the square. Four men stood there hunched together, fiddling with little bags. I saw them before they saw me. I kept looking straight ahead towards the junction, and you did the same. But then one of them stepped into my field of vision. I had time to note the way he shifted over his shoulder bag, and that the visor of his cap was pushed down so far that it covered his eyebrows. He stepped into the cycle lane and I met his eyes. He stopped. I recognized him as a student from Bellevue High School, whom I'd worked with about a year earlier. I couldn't remember his name. But he remembered mine: 'Hey, Nick!' he said. 'Hey, brother!' I said and pedalled on.

When we came to the house, a four-storey apartment block, there was nothing to see. All the windows had been replaced.

All the debris had been cleared away. We couldn't get into the stairwell. A piece of cordon tape fluttering from a tree was the only indication that something had happened here.

55

Mark called and said that Bullis had pulled out. 'They didn't have the money,' he said. 'They really wanted to take Elijah, but they didn't realize they had to put up all the funds.'

'I didn't want to play there anyway,' you said grimly when we met in the square after school and I told you the news.

Fourteen days have now passed since the explosion. More information has gone out to the public. The boy is still being kept sedated, apparently. He has lost some limbs, a leg and a hand, and he may possibly be blind, but his condition is described as stable.

Three days ago you spoke to Abbe on the telephone. It was a long and gloomy call, you told me. He'd called you from his residential facility. He said he loathed his situation; he could no longer play basketball or go to Malmö and meet his family and friends. You'd even spoken about Josef. Abbe had confirmed that it was Josef who'd blown himself up.

The first few hours after finding out you were much the same as ever. Several times you said: 'You see, Nick. What did I tell you?' But then you grew taciturn, and you stayed close to me. In the days that followed, apart from when you were at school, we spent every hour together.

I feel nothing at all. As soon as the sense of unease comes over me, I project it at the arseholes who led him into this, or his peers, or the institutions, or Sweden, or himself. I have no feelings of guilt. If I had taken care of him as I'm taking care of you, I would have changed his life. He would then not have blown himself up. I'm well aware of this. But I feel no guilt.

As always when the spring sun first emerges, there was a festival atmosphere around Möllan Square. I bought a bag of pears, we took a seat under the *Dignity of Labour* statue, and we looked around. A group of young men who, judging by their manner, hairstyles and dress code, were recent arrivals in Sweden, milled about in loosely constituted groups. They were all aged between eighteen and twenty-five, and their purpose for being there was unclear. I often thought that the men, who kept a low profile, smoking and talking, chose the square because the place had an anonymizing effect; here, you could be anyone you wished to be, look any way you wished to look without attracting attention to yourself, or being out of place. You can sell junk here, more or less openly, without having to worry about someone calling the police. You can just stand about yelling. Like the hipsters who occupied the far end of the square, you can sit or lie down – maybe even fuck in public – on dirty blankets, drink beer, play music, sing, or sleep, be semi-naked, without any raising of eyebrows. This is our place in the world. We have spent time here more or less every day since you moved in. Just passing through, to eat, make some purchases, or chill out. It was here that I met Josef the last time. It must have been at about the time he was taken into care.

You don't want to talk about Josef. You don't want to talk about anything. Since you found out, since you had your fears confirmed, you withdraw as often as you can. You lie on the sofa watching YouTube, you listen to music, or you read. Silent and introspective.

Any talk about the USA, or speculation about how the two remaining schools may approach things, also seems quite pointless. We know nothing and we have no control over what will happen. I feel stupid for tricking you into what feels more and more like some sort of craftily assembled spectacle. For not preparing you more for the seduction strategies of the teams, the schools, the agents. We devoured everything, skin and bones and all. Especially you. Because you're a child. Easily fooled and divorced from reality.

One of the bright lights of your life is Jessica. You talk on the telephone several times per day, and when I eavesdrop on you, your voices are sweetly confidential. You say that things are going to work themselves out with one of the schools, God has made a decision about it, the USA is your destiny. Jessica is patient with your long monologues. She offers interjections and leaves space for silence. And when you change the subject, you're the one who's supportive, insightful and sensitive. Yesterday, after you'd stayed silent for an hour in your bed, you said: 'You know what, Nick. Jessica looks like my future wife. One day I'll marry her. We'll have beautiful brown kids.'

Jessica is your first real love. But she lives in Stockholm. It'll never work.

56

Showan has come out of his coma. His condition is no longer life-threatening. But if – and how well – he recovers remains to be seen. News of his assault has spread everywhere. Showan has become a symbol of anti-fascism and anti-racism. All over the world, the hashtag #kämpashowan – Fight Showan – is being shared, with pictures of people holding up signs in support.

It's a powerful feeling; it's actually quite surreal. Malmö and Möllan and our friend have dropped into the international spotlight.

Ten thousand people have gathered in the square in Möllan to demonstrate. And we stood in the middle of the crowd.

It was the first demonstration I've ever taken part in, and the biggest one in Malmö in modern times. The feeling of unity was irresistible. You also felt yourself getting involved. It wasn't the usual collective. These were people from all social strata: left-wing organizations with uniform clothes and masked faces, families with children, wage slaves, average Malmö residents and others who'd come in from other parts of Sweden and Denmark. Slogans rumbled like tidal waves across the square. Torches and smoke flares burned and, against a lit-up lead-grey sky, Showan's face was held aloft on flags and placards. You raised your fist into the air, grimaced angrily, and shouted out loudly. *Anti-fascism is self-defence! Fight on Malmö! Fuck racism! Fuck the Sweden Democrats!*

That Showan would survive made us stronger; it intensified our fury even more. And that Josef had almost died, but would survive, somehow overwhelmed us further. It was epic but also comedic. Every time I was about to shout out something, I swallowed my words. They just didn't come out. I opened my mouth and blushed and laughed at myself. There was something lovely about it, nostalgic. It was new. I thought about my godlessness, the connection I had been lacking my whole life. The sense of togetherness here was so beautiful. Then we went home.

Just before midnight came an SMS from Mark: **Sorry, guys. Episcopal has declined. They didn't say why. They just said it couldn't be done. Now we just have to hope that Goretti delivers.**

You were lying in bed, reading. I stood next to you and told you. You didn't take your eyes off the page you were reading, you just said: 'Thanks, Nick.'

'Are you okay?' I asked.

'Yeah,' you said. 'I think Goretti are going to say yes. They liked me. I have a feeling about it. *Inshallah.*'

'Yeah,' I said. 'Let's hope.'

57

Jessica is the one who keeps your mood up. I don't have the capacity to do it. But something is wrong. Yesterday she sent a text, and when you read it out to me there was an anxiety in your voice. It was difficult that you could never meet, she wrote. To such a degree that she felt she had to distance herself from you, in order to stop herself feeling bad.

I'd made the mistake of involving myself in your relationship, counselling you in how to make it work. I'd told you it was probably not sensible trying to decide too much over the telephone, planning for the future, pronouncing yourselves boyfriend/girlfriend, when in fact you'd hardly even met. Which sounded sensible, you thought, and I heard you repeating the words to Jessica: 'Maybe it's better if we don't decide a lot of stuff and kill off the relationship that way. You have to see each other if you want to be together.'

Now she's setting the boundaries, pushing you away, and it's worrying you.

'It hurts so much that I can't see her, Nick,' you said one night after you'd gone to bed. You looked so pitiful as you explained, with much emotion, how you loved this girl, whose importance for you seems to keep growing in her absence.

But then you bounced up in a thrashing movement. 'Maybe there's a way of solving it, Nick,' you blurted out. 'Maybe I can go to Stockholm to visit her. It doesn't cost much. I can save up all I've got.'

'But you don't have anything,' I said, with a smile.

'But, okay,' you said. 'I can get the money, I promise, and it only takes a couple of hours on the train to get there.'

You sat on the edge of the bed, filled with eagerness. 'What do you say, Nick? You think we can solve it?'

'Course we can,' I said. 'But it all depends on whether Jessica wants to, and that her mum agrees to it.'

'Of course she does!' you said, slightly offended. 'We've already spoken about it. But, honest, you think it would work?'

'Yes,' I repeated. 'But you'll have to take a Friday off if you're going for the weekend. And talk to your coach about missing games.'

'It's cool,' you said. 'You said yourself, love is the most important thing. So it's an easy choice.'

'That's settled, then,' I said.

This was no good. Once again I'd poked around in things that were none of my business, encouraging something that was doomed to fail. Maybe I should have said that her distancing manoeuvres were a bad sign, that you'd be better off giving her some time and space. But this would just be another way of sticking my nose in.

I went into the kitchen to heat up a carton of food from the Greek.

I heard your worked-up voice from the living room. You'd called Jessica.

And right there I understood why you were in such an impatient rush to see her. You'd come to the same conclusion as me: she was on her way out of your life. She didn't want anything to do with you.

58

After keeping his silence for almost a month, Mark got in touch with an inscrutable exhortation: if we hurried up about producing the correct papers from your school, certificates and converted report cards stamped with the school's seal, and in addition if we solved the issue of the student visa, there was a possible opening.

'Are we talking about a different school?' I asked. I'd already given up any thought of Goretti.

'No,' said Mark. 'Goretti have said that they may be able to solve the cost, the full grant. It's far from a done deal, though. They described it as "a slight brightening" in the application.'

'What does "a slight brightening" imply?' I asked, sounding more insolent than I meant to.

'It means that they may be able to solve the costs,' he said, 'that they've found a possible sponsor.'

'Okay,' I said. 'That's good news.'

'Well,' he said. 'It's probably a long shot. And regardless of that, there's the outstanding problem of finding a family to lodge with. But we have to start somewhere, we have nothing to lose.'

'No,' I said, muttering in Swedish: 'You don't, anyway.'

And so began a long, bureaucratic process.

First, I had to talk to your mother, inform her of the situation and what had to be done. I called her one afternoon while you were at school. I was in a cold sweat. The signals rang through and she answered, sounding unexpectedly chirpy. I told her that we had to meet with the head at your school and fix the papers, even though the chances of your being awarded a full grant were absolutely minimal.

'Okay,' she said cooperatively. 'Just tell me what I need to do and consider it done.'

Our call was brief, but a warm feeling lingered inside after we'd hung up. She'd sounded so carefree, your mother. Happy. It was our first ever normal conversation.

Two days later we hugged one another outside the head's office. Your mother was nervous and tentative. And she was exactly as I remembered her: a bright essence. That you love her and miss her is something I can truly understand.

We were welcomed by the head, a mild-mannered, middle-aged woman whose name I have forgotten. Her room was like an oasis in a chaos of children: muted lighting, the sun coming through the blinds in gentle streaks, the muffled voices outside like sounds from underwater.

We introduced ourselves. I said in my usual, slightly apologetic manner that I was here in my capacity as your coach, someone who was close to the family. Your mother didn't say a great deal. She nodded, asked a couple of questions, but mainly just sat quietly with her handbag on her knees. It was good to be there with her. As if we made up a sort of team whose task it was to make your dreams come true.

In less than a week I had the right papers in my mailbox. I forwarded them to Mark, he thanked me. And after that I haven't heard from him.

Things went less smoothly with Jessica. After you'd been planning the trip to Stockholm for three days and I'd bought you a cheap train ticket, Jessica called to blow off the plans.

'I'm sorry, I can't see you, Elijah,' she said. 'It's not going to work . . . because it's Mum's birthday and I have to get things ready for the party. And then I have games as well this weekend. And my friends are coming over.'

59

On the legal graffiti wall by the dealers' roundabout in Möllan, the gigantic artwork with the words *Fight Showan*, added after the attack, has become a sort of site of pilgrimage for people who want to remember, mourn, look for strength and take photographs. Even though we lived so close to it we'd never paid it a visit. Today that was going to change, we decided, and so after lunching we strolled over.

When we got there, we found not only the artwork, but also Showan himself in the middle of the roundabout, surrounded by friends. He was holding a water bottle in his right hand and there was a sort of rugby helmet on his head. His friends were in high spirits, raising beer bottles aloft, while Showan looked vacant.

It was like seeing a ghost, and I suddenly grew nervous.

Maybe I was afraid that he wouldn't recognize me. And that the feelings I'd experienced – my sorrow about a friend subjected to a murder attempt by Nazis, my happiness that he survived it, and my total immersion in the uproar and tension that had been stirred up – would be rejected. Maybe I thought that his celebrity would have an effect on our friendship, and he'd be uncomfortable about yet another 'friend' wanting something out of him, hugging him and being emotionally expressive.

I didn't want to be that friend. Never again did I want to express strong feelings for another human being, in the belief that they were mutual, only to feel stupid and ashamed of myself later when I realized I'd misjudged our level of familiarity.

The last thing I'd heard about Showan was that he'd had to have three new operations. Half of his skull bone had been replaced with a plastic sheet held in place by screws. I'd heard that his memory was affected, especially his short-term memory, and that he was in a rehabilitation centre, and that people who knew him, who'd met with him, said that he wasn't the same, his personality was changed.

'Is that him?' you burst out, pointing at Showan and his entourage. 'That's Showan, isn't it, Nick?'

A couple of his friends looked over at us, not without a certain animosity.

Shit, I thought.

'Yeah,' I said in an unnaturally loud voice. I smiled: 'Sure as hell that's Shosho!'

Showan didn't move a muscle in his face when we stepped onto the roundabout.

'How're things, Shosho?' I said. I stopped a few metres away from him. 'Damn good to see you, brother. How are you?'

Showan gave me an enervated look, his face as droopy as a hangdog. Then he scrunched up his eyes, as if searching his memory. But no. I was a stranger to him.

I said: 'It was good to see you, my friend. We have to move on now. Take care of yourselves.'

We turned around to leave.

'Nico,' said Showan in a gravelly voice, and cleared his throat. He put his head askance.

'Yeah,' I said, and was moved.

He held out his arms and we embraced.

'Sorry, brother,' he said. 'My head's so fucking slow. Screw loose, you know. It's really good to see you too.'

60

It's 01.23. On a Sunday. In front of me, in the camp bed which makes a slight squeaking sound every time you inhale, you've been asleep for the past two hours. All I can see of you is the top of your frizzy head and your disproportionally long toes, which stick out at the end of the bed.

You've grown several centimetres in a short period of time. These days you're taller than me – and I never hear the end of it: 'Nick, now I'm two centimetres taller! Now three! Check this, Nick – five!'

But there'll be no buying of new beds for your fast-growing body. You will no longer be living with me.

We got the word yesterday. And now when I think of it, think of the way the phone made a pinging sound, and I saw that it was an email from Mark, and I opened it to have a read, I can't for the life of me remember where we were. Sitting on the front steps outside the Johannes church? On the bench in the shoot-up park outside the flat? Or were we on foot, maybe, walking back from the grocery store, the Greek or Möllan?

The place is erased from my memory, but not the sunlight flowing over us, the strong light reflecting against the glass

screen of the mobile phone, which I shaded with my cupped
hand while at the same time zooming in closer to the subject
line: *See attached file*. And Mark's message: *Goretti is on. And
everything is solved. Elijah is moving to the USA! :)* Then, the
attached PDF document with the small, hard-to-read letters.

And I remember the joy. The joy that made your eyes tear
up. And made us both jump around like crazies, hugging
each other, laughing and shrieking.

At the top left of the document, the school's logo had
been pasted in: St Maria Goretti High School. And then
your full name: Elijah Marcus Clarance.

Dear Elijah,

    **It is the distinct honor of the Admissions Committee
to inform you that you have been accepted as a
sophomore member at St Maria Goretti High School. It is
with genuine sincerity that we extend our congratulations
to you and your family, and our best wishes for your
future as a member of the Goretti family.**

It was impossible to take it in.

For the rest of the day, we hardly mentioned it at all. We
haven't said very much about it today either. Now and then
we exchange smiles, laugh right out, hug each other, blurt
out emotional reactions: 'Shit . . . God . . . Can you get your
head around it . . . ? I just can't . . .'

It was as if we were sitting on a piece of news of global
significance.

And actually, we were: after all, you'd been offered a full

scholarship to play basketball, study and live in Hagerstown, Maryland, USA.

It was fucking wicked and unreal, which was how you put it once you found the words.

But what about accommodation?

Mark said earlier that they'd made a sweep of the whole town of Hagerstown in their efforts to find a family with which you could lodge. Judging by earlier conversations, I'd understood that living on your own was out of the question. For financial reasons, but also because it put too much of a burden of responsibility on you and was therefore also too much of a risk for the school.

I didn't want to bring this up and ruin the atmosphere, so I waited until you were asleep before I called Mark. It was early evening at his end, he was busy with the washing-up and he had yelling children in the background.

He cried out: 'We did it, Nick. We found Elijah a good family. They were in the military, they're retired Marines. So things will be kept orderly, which will do him good.'

'That's fantastic news,' I said. 'He'll manage it without any problems.'

I filled up with three surging emotions inside: a sense of happiness that it was all done, the obstacles had been pushed aside and you were moving to the USA. A dull sadness because you were leaving me. And then, anxiety about what Mark had just told me: *retired Marines.*

How would this work out? You, who'd never cooked your own food and hardly cleaned up or did your laundry or tidied away your things; who guzzled your food noisily, and farted and took a shit with the toilet door left open. How would you handle the strict American approach, the authoritarian relationship between adults and children?

I decided not to give it another thought. If there's one thing you've shown these last few years, it's how quickly you adapt and develop – completely shapeshift yourself, even.

Just as I was about to express my gratitude to Mark, he interrupted me.

'There's one thing I want to tell you, Nick,' he said. 'One second . . .'

He left the kitchen, and the loud din was replaced by distant birdsong as he pulled the veranda door shut. 'What I'm going to tell you must not under any circumstances be revealed to Elijah. The school and I have agreed that he won't be told anything about this until he's graduated. I hope you can respect that.' He was silent for a few seconds, and then he said: 'Do you remember the caretaker at Goretti? The elderly man who kept the players supplied with balls?'

'Yeah,' I said, 'I remember him.'

The man, who was in his eighties, had caught my attention with his stooped back, busying himself with various tasks in the sports hall. His age had made me curious, so I'd asked Mark who he was. Mark had replied that he'd been retired for many years, but he'd once been a student at the school. Mark went on: 'He's the one who's financing Elijah's stay in the USA. He's the one who's making Elijah's dreams come true.'

'What?' I blurted out. 'How do you mean?'

'Well, I mean exactly what I just said,' said Mark. 'He's paying for everything. He has a big heart, he wants to give something back to the school, which he can do in this way, and give a young person the opportunity he once had.'

'I just can't believe it,' I said, feeling my emotions building up in my throat. 'That's two hundred thousand kronor per year, six hundred thousand in three years. Out of his own pocket! For a kid he doesn't even know. It's impossible!'

Mark laughed. 'Yeah, it's pretty amazing. Anyway, that's how it is. Elijah is blessed. In all my years I've never seen anything like it.'

61

If spring was our darkest time together, with our hopes of your move to the USA waning, the attempted murder of Showan, Josef's accident, your injured foot and Jessica, the early summer has been the brightest time.

Everything is happening at a blistering pace.

Yesterday you went to prom. You were dressed in my funeral suit, my white shirt, a crimson bow tie and handkerchief, and a dusted-off grey-black hat, which we found on the shelf in the wardrobe.

You had no date, you told me. 'But it doesn't matter, Nick. I'm going with my ball!'

You were like a thirties gangster, posing there against the kitchen wall with your slightly mischievous smile, your hat tilted and the ball under your arm. I took several photos.

'You're looking stylish, little brother,' I said, taking some more photos. 'Nothing surprising about that. You're dressed like me.'

I went with you to the front door, helped you get into my black overcoat, and folded up the collar.

'Damn,' I said, giving you a hug. 'You'll have to give your ball a proper name if people ask who your date is.'

'Easy,' you said, looking down at the overcoat and buttoning it up with one hand, as you had just learned to do.

'I'll always dress like this when I'm a pro, Nick,' you said. 'But then I won't be wearing your clothes, 'cos by then you'll be too short.'

I lingered in the doorway listening to your clattering steps as you disappeared down the stairs.

'Nick!' you called out, just as I was about to close the door. 'Jessica!'

'What do you mean?' I said. 'What about Jessica?'

'That's what I'll call it. The ball, I mean. The ball's going to be called Jessica!'

62

SVT called and wanted to broadcast a story on us. The reporter said that initially she'd wanted to interview me about my work with young people, but then she got wind of a story about a boy dribbling his way around Möllan, and how we were very close. 'I've heard a lot about your strong connection,' she said, 'and I think it could make a very interesting piece.'

I went completely cold. What had she heard? Why was she interested in us?

I said that you and I would have to talk about it. And that she could also just email me her thoughts and questions. 'No problem,' she said. 'It will probably be fairly light-hearted. There's a big interest in this type of story.'

My reaction was one of fear. I felt that nothing that was private could be revealed. You took the absolute opposite view.

'We have to tell them everything! How you took care of me, and about our struggle, and Mum. I want us to be a hundred per cent real, Nick, and say it just like it is.'

'You'd regret that,' I said. 'But I guess it's okay if we talk about our relationship and your dreams.'

'Okay,' you said. 'As you like. As long as we're a hundred per cent real.'

The first filming location was in Möllan Square. The camera guy toddled along behind you as you dribbled along over the cobblestones, wearing your T-shirt with SWEDEN written across the chest. The sun was shining, lots of people had stopped to watch you showing off your skills. After that, they filmed you in your classroom and interviewed me outside the school entrance. The reporter said that the programme, which would be both aired on TV and streamed online, would probably be watched by more than a million viewers. That didn't make me any less nervous. And I knew that the slightest error in what I said, the slightest misstep, could be misinterpreted, and this caused me a good deal of anguish.

Things went well at the start. I kept it formal; I talked about the first time I met you at the Malmö Festival. The cocky kid challenging his elders. But then something happened. Standing there, sharing memories, which no one else had ever heard about, with a reporter, in front of a camera and a million-strong audience, made me emotional, and then I heard myself say: 'He's like a younger brother to me. I love him as if he was a part of my own family.'

After the interview I called the reporter and said that the bit about my loving the kid came out wrong, it might be subject to misinterpretation, please do take it out.

'No problem,' she said abruptly. 'We can cut that out.'

The last filming location was an outdoor court. The camera

crew circled us while we took shots at the basket and talked, and after that they put some questions to you.

You said, as you usually do, that you were going to become the best in the world and play in the NBA, predictable answers from a Malmö kid with hubris. But then, when they asked you what I meant to you, it was as if your self-confidence drained out of you, and you turned serious and started stammering.

'Nick is someone who's always been there for me like a brother . . . No, no, I want to try that again, that wasn't good. It has to be a hundred per cent real.'

You walked away from the camera and took a few deep breaths.

'Okay . . . Nick's been like a father to me, a big brother. Nick has helped me with everything. We have a really strong relationship.'

We sat in front of the TV when the report was aired.

To my horror, they hadn't removed the sequence where I said I loved you. I panicked. I kept my feelings to myself, but they tore at me.

'This is huge, Nick,' you said grandly, once it was over. You had tears in your eyes. 'This is fucking huge. Now Sweden knows, the whole of Sweden. Now they can't deny us.'

Afterwards I watched the clip online several times. Did I seem like a weirdo? No. I didn't think so. It felt sincere.

To celebrate our now being 'celebrities in the whole of Sweden' (your words) we had triple portions at Chicken Cottage. Our mood was tip-top. We spoke about the USA, and what this change would mean.

'It'll be a big challenge, Elijah,' I said.

'It's cool, I'll manage.'

'No,' I said. 'You can't take it as easily as that. You'll be living with ex-Marines and you're going to a private school with strict rules and dress codes. It's going to put a lot of demands on you. It'll be in a different stratosphere from your current hippie life. With me you can just come and go any way you like. You take a shit and piss with the door open. All that's over now.'

You laughed so hard that there were bits of food flying about in the air.

'I'm serious,' I said. 'It makes me nervous.'

'But it's no big deal, Nick,' you said. 'Of course I'll manage.'

'There's no *of course* about it,' I said. 'The fact is, you're living a life of bloody luxury here and you've got used to it. We eat out in a restaurant every day, you never have to do anything in the apartment, I give you cash whenever you need it – everything is dished out for you.'

You lowered your eyes.

'It's not your fault, bro,' I said. 'It's not even wrong. I've chosen to have things this way. I just mean it's important for you to make a mental reset now. Your approach from now on has got to be different.'

'Mmm,' you mumbled.

'What I'm trying to tell you is, you'll be smoked out head first if you fuck up. That's how strict they are over there. Yanks are nuts.'

'I understand,' you said. 'I just have to do it.'

Edvin, the cook, who must have been listening to our conversation, came up to our table. He smiled without saying anything, then held out a bottle over your whole, almost charred chickens, drenching them in hot sauce.

'Thanks, bro,' you said. Then your forehead pulled into a worried frown. 'But what do I do, then, to stop myself from fucking up?'

'Here,' I said, pulling a napkin from the dispenser and handing over a pen. 'Let's start with you writing down the things that you think you need to keep in mind when you're with your host family. For example, how you need to behave yourself around the table at mealtimes. Okay?'

You put the pen in your mouth, thought about it for a moment, then you wrote:

1. Eat with my mouth shut.

2. No elbows on the table.

3. Never reach across anyone.

4. Ask for it instead.

5. Don't pick food off someone's plate.

6. Never eat with fingers.

7. If I pour myself a drink, ask the others if they want some.

8. Never ever smack my lips.

'This is a very good start, brother,' I said. 'A lot of important points here.'

'But how strict are they at this school?' you asked. 'This thing about the dress code. It can't be any worse than having to wear a jacket and, like, a good sweater.'

'I really don't know,' I said. 'We can check online.'

By clicking on the tab for *uniform code* on Goretti's home page, I opened a PDF file, and we were able to read the rules applicable to boys at the school. During the whole school day one had to wear a white or, in exceptional cases, light blue, properly ironed shirt. It had to be tucked into one's trouser lining, so that the belt, which had to be brown or black, was visible. The T-shirt under the shirt had to be plain white, without a printed design. All students had to wear khaki trousers. The trouser leg couldn't drag along the ground, and must not be worn cut-off, or frayed. One could not have tattoos. One was not allowed to draw on one's skin. And so it went on, for another two sides of A4. There were even rules for the distance between the fringe and the eyebrows.

63

On the way home from the restaurant we ran into Rahim. He was walking in our direction. He was happy, telling us he'd just got engaged to the love of his life. Soon there'd be a big party.

We kept company down Smedjegatan, turned right into Södra Förstadsgatan, and outside the ICA supermarket I caught sight of Anja and her son. Her arm was linked with his. They looked like they were waiting for a lift. But when our eyes met, she hurried across the street. We hugged each other. She looked at you, then she turned to her boy.

'You must be the same age,' she said.

'I'm almost sixteen,' you said.

'Yeah, see!' said Anja. 'He is too. His name is Noah.'

'My name's Elijah,' you said.

'How are you?' she said, with a smile at me. 'Shit, you got so skinny.' She gave me a shove on the shoulder.

'Really?' I said. 'Even though I eat like a pig? Things are fine with me. What about yourself?'

'I'm well,' she said with a shrug. 'Like, did you know I often think about your mother? I miss her like hell, Nick, she was like an angel in my life.'

'Yeah,' I said. 'She really was, I miss her too.'

We hugged again. Anja hugged you too. Said goodbye.

Anja was off the wall as usual, the way I remember her from my childhood. But she seemed worn down. Difficult to put one's finger on exactly what it was, but she didn't seem to be in a good place.

When we came home you asked about my mother. Anja's remark, when she so directly brought up the subject, opened the door. I had told you earlier that my mother was dead and had also said a little about her, what she was like as a person, and that she was often in my thoughts. Now, we sat up until half past two at night. I told you everything. About my mother, my brother, my growing up, about love, how lonely I had been, how frightened I had been. And still am. But also, how happy.

'I've lived a damn good life, Elijah,' I said. 'I love to be alive.'

And I told you about my father. Answered your questions with honesty.

'Dad left, brother,' I said. 'He's alive. He exists here in the world. He just doesn't want to be here with me.'

64

A mentor at your school saw the programme on SVT. She was moved by it, and now she wants to introduce her sister to me. You came home all eager about it. You stood outside the bathroom door while I lay in the bath, and you raised your voice to make yourself heard over the sound of running water.

'I thought, she's got to be talking smack,' you blathered on. 'I told her "Nick's pretty picky, that's why he hasn't got anyone. He's waiting for The One." But then she showed a photo of her sister and you would have thought she was beautiful. I promise, Nick, don't mess this one up. She's really nice, and a doctor too.'

I turned off the water. 'Mmm,' I said. 'But I'm not comfortable with you trying to be the matchmaker.'

'I'm not,' you said. 'It was her sister who showed me the photo. But I know what I saw. You're going to thank me.'

Fifteen minutes later I got out of the tub. Wrapped a towel around my body and went into the hall. There you stood, still in your outdoor clothes, fidgeting with your phone.

'Here,' you said. You held up the photo that your mentor had sent you.

'I'm telling you,' you said.

'Yeah,' I said. 'She's really beautiful. But no thanks, I'm not interested.'

65

Yesterday you got your final grades. Out of breath, you stood in the kitchen holding up the laminated document.

'Look, Nick!'

You'd improved in all the subjects.

'It's thanks to you, Nick,' you said. 'You always said it's important to know things and to own your knowledge. And yeah, it's also down to Malcolm X and K-O, of course.'

In a report, a teacher wrote that you had gone through an academic transformation. From being an annoying, cocky type (she didn't put it like that – she wrote that you had concentration issues) to someone who was genuinely motivated to learn about things and share what you knew. She wrote that you actively took part in the lessons and raised your voice about things you did not agree with.

'This is entirely your own achievement,' I said. Then I put my hand on your shoulder. 'Do you know I'm proud of you?'

'Yeah, Nick,' you said.

'I really mean it, Elijah. I've never been so proud of anyone in my whole life. Congratulations!'

*   *   *

You seem to want to top up as many memories as possible from your home city before you move out. So in the last few weeks we've put a lot of time into making excursions.

The destination today was Slottsparken. I'd told you there was a place with some hidden traces from bombs that fell during the Second World War. We cycled through the lush greenery, past the half-naked bodies in the grass; we heard the trumpeting of geese from across the pond, and the gravel crunching under our wheels. The sun stood high in the sky, striking sparks from the surface of the water, so blinding that we had to look away.

'There!' I said when I caught sight of the bridge.

It was smaller than I remembered it, just a couple of metres long, built across a purling stream. You skidded to a halt, quickly got off your bike, and went to locate the hollow.

'Caused by shrapnel,' I said. 'There were three bombs in all. They shredded trees into splinters, left big craters in the ground, and shattered windows in apartments hundreds of metres away. But the only thing left of all that devastation is that little hole.'

I moved my hand along the side of the granular railing.

'Feel here,' I said. 'It's here. It's not a big hole but you can feel it quite clearly.'

'Yeah, shit,' you said, poking your finger into the hole. 'So sick. Just think that there were bombs falling on Malmö.'

After that we sat down with burgers by the grill opposite the City Library, watching the people coming and going. Two ducks came waddling along, snuffling at the air. You tore off a piece of bread, split it in two and tossed it to them.

'Shall we?' I said.

'I think so,' you said, getting out your notepad from your bag.

'How does it feel now that the trip is getting closer?' I asked.

'It feels good, Nick,' you said. 'But I'm going to miss Malmö and I'm going to miss you. A lot of time has passed, bro. We've become like a little family.'

You drew the ballpoint pen up and down in the margin until the black ink came out. Then you wrote and underlined: *Packing for USA.*

'Have you ever been worried about me, Nick?' you asked, looking at me.

'Yes,' I answered. 'I've always worried about you.'

'What's made you worried?'

'Everything,' I said. 'I've worried that you won't make it. That you'll end up in the shit. That society will hurt you. That you'll die. I've been afraid that you'll intrude on my personal life. Before you moved in, I was living on my own. I suppose I've been afraid of losing myself, afraid of being abandoned. That was the thing that made me treat you badly now and then. I've got a lot of guilt about that.'

'But that's not true,' you said. 'You never hurt me, Nick. That's what's so insane. You've always been so kind, even when I didn't deserve it. When were you ever bad to me?'

'For example, when I let you sleep on the couch for a long time,' I said. 'Sometimes, by being hard and cold. A lot of things like that.'

'But it's not true,' you said. 'I don't know anyone who would have done what you did. Especially not for someone like me, a *blatte* from Nydala. And I've often thought it must be hard to have me there smacking my lips when I eat and disturbing you when you're trying to read and asking about money all the time. But I'm so grateful for all the things you've done for me. Sometimes I think like Anja, what she said about your mother that time we met her on Möllan. You're an angel in my life. Who's there to make sure everything turns out well. Because it wasn't like that before. I've been so worried about myself, afraid that I won't find the right way, afraid that I'm going to end up a bum like all the others. I felt there was no place for me, no one wanted anything to do with me. And that's how it was. No one wanted anything to do with me.'

'What if it's the other way round,' I said, meeting your gaze head on, 'and *you're* the angel in *my* life?'

One of the ducks was now by your feet, nibbling on your shoelaces to catch your attention. You flinched.

'I don't have any more, *habibi*,' you said in a baby voice. 'All the bread's finished.'

You held out your hand. I clasped it. We embraced.

'You and me for ever, Nick,' you said.

'For ever,' I said.

You put the pad on your knee, lifted your pen to write something. Then, you stopped yourself.

'But listen, Nick . . . if you're more open to love now and all that, then you have to find the courage to make contact with people, even if it's not all serious and shit.'

'How do you mean?' I asked, even though I knew what you were going to say.

'That one, the doctor, for example. You could just drop her a line. You said yourself she was fine.'

I laughed. 'Don't start that again. I'm not going to contact someone I never even met in real life.'

'But, Nick, you can just add her on Facebook. It's not like some big deal. If you add her, I promise I'll stop going on about it. Okay?'

'You promise?' I said.

'I swear,' you said. 'You won't hear anything else about it.'

I picked up my telephone, went into her Facebook profile. Amna was her name. She was twenty-nine years old, recently graduated as a medical doctor. Her profile picture was a selfie, a blurred photo taken with a granular filter. She had a side parting, dark brown hair, brown eyes, and was very beautiful.

'Add her now, Nick,' you said, glaring at me. I clicked on Add Friend.

'There,' I said. 'It's done. No more nagging now. Okay? Now let's get your list finished.'

On the way home the sun was going down. When we passed the Malmö Opera it shone over the angular building, spilling across the sky in orange, blue and purple.

A third of what you needed to pack belonged to me: clothes, headphones, books, aftershave. It was a rich source of consolation. These were things that would remind you of us, of me, of our time together.

I thought about how, soon enough, you'd outgrow the clothes, the headphones would break, and the aftershave would run out. It was a sad thought, loaded with symbolism. I was still convinced that our relationship – even if we maintained our contact – from now on would gradually be changed, become more formal, less intense, and emptied of emotions.

'I have to take a dump,' I said, as we turned into Möllevångsgatan, just a few metres from the flat. 'Can you fix the food?'

I gave you two hundred-kronor banknotes. You swung your handlebars over and disappeared around the corner. I leaned my bicycle against the house wall.

I sat in the kitchen and looked out at the sky. The orange notes were now completely dissolved into nuances of purple. Higher up they shifted into dark blue and this would remain so for the rest of the night, never turning completely black, sprinkled with faintly shimmering stars.

The telephone rang. It was Rahim.

I answered, which I knew was a bad idea.

He sounded like he was speeding.

'Something terrible has happened,' he said. 'A boy has died, a teenager. But we don't know him. He was stabbed in the throat with a knife or a bottle. It happened in Oxie. There were a lot of kids there.'

'What do you know about him? Do you have a name?'

'No. But Sandra was there afterwards, just before the police left the scene. She said a name that I can't remember, something Spanish I think, but I don't know for sure. It's not one of our kids anyway.'

'Okay,' I said. 'Maybe someone can get themselves over there, hang out for a bit.'

'Yes,' said Rahim. 'I'll take the car. Bring Sandra and Ladi with me. Call you when I know more.'

66

Amna writes on Messenger: **My sister is too funny . . . She said that someone was going to add me on Facebook and I definitely had to accept, ha-ha. You had some similar demands I'm assuming?**

I answer: **Ha-ha, yeah, one could say that. But it was more like my life was threatened if I didn't add you as a friend. They seem to have it all planned out. Maybe they'll calm down if I ask you out for a coffee?**

Amna answers: **I think so. Just tell me where and when is good for you.**

We decided to meet at Lilla Plaza one evening later in the week. I turned up a little before the appointed time, wanted to see her before she saw me.

The evening was warm, outside tables everywhere were full, the underlying sound levels were high. She arrived on a bicycle. Her hair was curly, and it moved in the wind. She wore a long black coat, black trousers and high black boots. She got off, chained her bicycle to a lamp post and moved towards the centre of the square. I followed behind and moved in closer from the side. Her hair was fairer than I had expected, her skin browner, as if she'd just been abroad.

I grew insecure. Traipsed along a few metres behind her to one side, and had time to think to myself that this would probably be a disaster. And that it was stupid of me to put on a polo-neck top.

'Amna?' I said with a smile, jutting my head forward in that ridiculous way when one tries to catch the attention of a stranger.

We decided on Moosehead Bar. The bartender was a young man I'd worked with but hadn't seen in several years.

'Nick,' he called out when we stepped into the throng of people. 'Damn good to see you! What are you doing in these upmarket parts?'

He hugged me, then turned to Amna and said: 'I mean, this geezer . . . he's one of the finest human beings I ever met.'

Amna laughed. 'Did you two arrange this in advance or what?'

The conversation flowed in an unforced manner for over three hours. The subjects varied: family, work, music, politics, children. Amna explained that she was a general practitioner, still unsure about specializing, but that in the future, for a couple of months per year, she wanted to work in the Horn of Africa. She radiated warmth and mildness; she seemed enthusiastic but collected, purposeful but rational. And, it seemed to me, curious about the dude sitting opposite her, slurping his fizzy drink. I looked at her, inspected her face. She had a thin scar under her left nostril, which made one think of harelips. Her chin was thin, almost pointed. She'd just been to Spain, she said. 'So nice to have some proper sun,' I said. And I thought to myself, as I sat there listening to her, that this was a face I could look at indefinitely. Or, as you once put it when speaking of Jessica: *she looks like my future wife.*

We parted ways. I stifled the rush of happiness that surged through me, and cycled up to the square, where a couple of friends were celebrating Mathi's thirtieth birthday. Mathi came stumbling out from Mascot's outside tables when he caught sight of me. He grinned from ear to ear. He was so drunk that he was trying to support himself against the air. He shouted out: 'How the hell was it, then? Did it feel good, or what's going on?'

'Yeah,' I said. 'I think I've found the one.'

'Serious?' he said.

'Yeah,' I said. 'That's how it felt, anyway.'

The rest of the guys followed behind him. They erupted into spontaneous dancing, glad about what they'd just heard, glad to be as drunk as lords. And by the time I withdrew, pushing my bicycle towards Södra Förstadsgatan, they'd forgotten I was ever there.

I passed the Greek on my right. The lights were out, the signs had been removed, the restaurant was closing. Chicken Cottage was also going to shut down. Last time we ate there, as I was waiting at the till to pay, Edvin said that the owners no longer saw much profitability in the venture.

'It's a pity,' he said, 'we had a lot of good years here.' He nodded at you. 'But he won't notice anything. When the next owner takes over here, he'll be in the US.'

You yelled as soon as I put the keys in the lock.

'What did I tell you! I promised you, Nick. And you're going to thank me later.' You burst out laughing. Your squeaky, shrill, enervating laugh. I laughed back at you.

67

Almost everything is prepared for your trip. The plane takes off in two weeks.

Yesterday, after visiting your mother to pick up some of your belongings, you came home and you were livid with anger. Three people unknown to you had been there, among them a woman who'd taken you aside and confided in you.

First, she said she'd heard a lot of good about you, that your mother was proud to have such a hardworking son as you. Then she talked about the murder on Oxie. She said that her son had been taken into custody, suspected on probable grounds for the deed.

'It's done,' she'd said, 'both for him and for me.'

The woman was drunk. She wept and hugged you, messed up your clothes. She said that this was the end, that none of them would ever recover themselves.

That her son had murdered another boy, who would not be recovering himself either, was not something she brought up.

You were shouting as you retold all this, so angry that you were panting. 'It's all so fucked up, Nick,' you said. 'Everything's just messed up all the time.'

I had just come home from my second date with Amna. We'd had dinner at Green Mango on Möllan and the atmosphere had been just as relaxed and nice as the last time around. The happiness was now punctured by what you were telling me.

You fell asleep early, just before eleven. I sat on the sofa, looking at you. *Two weeks, Elijah*, I thought. *That's how long you need to survive.*

68

Amna and I went to the cinema. I was nervous, I couldn't focus on the film. We munched from the same popcorn box. Giggled like teenagers, held hands. When the credits were rolling, I kissed her, and spilled my drink on the floor. You were waiting for us outside the cinema, leaning up against your bicycle. You lit up when you saw us. And even though it was the first time you and Amna had met, you gave each other a hug.

We pushed the bicycles home, you and me, in the drizzle. There was a low cloud cover hanging over the city, illuminated as if lit from within. You were happy, you were leaving Sweden very soon.

But there was a shadow hanging over you. You hadn't heard from your mother.

'She hasn't called me once,' you said, 'although she knows that I'm going. I can feel it, brother, I won't be seeing her before I kick off.

'Actually, I met Abbe earlier,' you continued. 'He was home on probation, I think. His eyes were completely black, Nick. He wasn't the same old funny *blatte* he used to be. He said you'd let him down. He said it several times: "Nick has let me down. Nick has let me down."'

'What did he mean by that?' I asked.

'He said you always used to be there for him. You were real to him when he was small, in the sports hall, at the Malmö Festival and all that. But then, like, you stopped being concerned about him, he said. As if you turned your back on him, let him down. He said you were just like all the others. But I defended you, of course. I said that's not right, Nick is real. He's taken care of me for two years. I've lived with him; he's done everything for me. That's what I said. But he just said: "Yeah, maybe he did all that for you. But not for me. He didn't give a damn about me."'

'You don't have to defend me, brother,' I said. 'Abbe is entitled to his feelings. And I can understand if he feels that way. Those are choices that I made. I couldn't take you all on, and it just naturally worked out in such a way that it was you.'

'Do you think Josef thought the same about you?' you asked, after a moment's silence. 'Did he also feel that you let him down?'

'Haven't got a clue,' I said. 'But it's possible. Yeah, it's even likely.'

69

The terminal at Copenhagen Airport was full of people, in spite of the early hour. Long queues wound back from the check-in desks and travellers hurried this way and that over the grey stone floor, pulling their heavy baggage behind them. Normally, it would have stressed me out. But just for once we were in good time, and we had more than two hours before the flight to Washington DC. I told myself that everything was under control.

Your packing was relatively modest, bearing in mind that it was a permanent move: a mid-size suitcase, a training bag, a rucksack, a bag containing a stash of chocolate and a book about Zlatan.

'You think I have everything?' you asked for the third time since we'd left the apartment.

'Yup,' I said. 'All your packing, all your papers. Calm down. Worst-case scenario is we left something really important, and you'll just have to stay in Malmö.'

You laughed. 'Yeah,' you said. 'It's not the worst thing that could happen. But honest, Nick. This is just insane. This is the dream. Like, how insane is this?!'

Since we got the information, the irrevocable decision that

you were going to move, I've thought a lot about this exact moment – our last moment together. I've worried that it'll feel unnatural, or that you'll suddenly have a change of heart, or even worse, that our farewell will feel stiff.

After checking in, with another half an hour before you needed to start moving towards passport control, we had breakfast. You ordered two bagels, half a cheese baguette and a hot chocolate. I had a coffee. We sat down by a gigantic glass facade with a view of the runway, where the aircrafts either rose towards or hurtled down from a morning-clear, pale sky.

'It's pretty unbelievable, isn't it,' I said, 'just how many planes you can fit into such a small space, and how they can keep a check on all the flights arriving and leaving, and in what direction, and how you never hear of miscalculations that have led to accidents at airports?'

'Yeah,' you said. 'It really is insane. But hey, Nick. When are you going to start giving me some cred for hooking you up with Amna?'

'Well,' I said, 'I would give you cred for it, if you didn't keep reminding me every fifteen minutes.'

'I'm proud of you anyway for having the guts to ask her out. That was really cool of you, brother.'

'Thanks,' I said. 'How are you feeling now ahead of your trip?'

'I was freaking out about it before,' you said. 'Because I thought it would be hard leaving you, going off, and maybe feeling lonely again. But I'm not worrying any more, because I know things are not going to be that way. We're going to stay tight even though we're in different countries.'

'Yeah,' I said. 'Of course. And it's not like we'll never see each other again.'

'But I guess the real question is, how are you going to manage without me?' you said. I laughed. 'How the hell are you going to manage without having some brat there, farting and munching and stealing your clothes?'

We drew closer to passport control. The pace here was calmer than in the terminal. Most of the travellers were pensioners, businesspeople talking on their phones, families with children.

'We're here, then,' I said.

'Yup,' you said. 'This is it.'

You hugged me. 'I love you, my brother,' you said. 'Thank you so much for all you've done for me, Nick. I really mean that.'

'It's me who should be thanking you, Elijah,' I said. 'This time we've had together has been the best of my life. I love you too.'

70

At the start of November, two months into the autumn term, you called me on Skype. Your smile lit up the screen. You were wearing your school uniform – white shirt, tie and a horrific navy blue cardigan. You said: 'We had our quarterly report today, Nick. You want to see?'

'No,' I said. 'My heart can't take any more disappointments from you.'

'So it's your lucky day,' you said, and with a grin on your face you held up the document in front of the camera.

'I got As and Bs in all the subjects,' you said. 'And not only that, check out what the teachers wrote about me.'

Very respectful. Actively participates in lessons. Cooperative and attentive.

Miss Keenan-Bartholomew had taken you aside when she personally handed over your school report and saluted you for your achievement. She said that few international students had reached your level in their first term, and she was so happy and proud to have you there.

But in the midst of our celebrations, as I also heaped praise on you, your face darkened. You said that you didn't want to kill the mood, but there was something horrible that you had to tell me.

'Have you heard about the murder and the attempted murder in Ekängen?' you asked.

'Yes,' I said. 'Of course. The media's full of it.'

'You know those guys were from Malmö, right?'

'Yeah,' I said. 'That was clear right from the word go.'

Two boys aged seventeen and sixteen had made their way to Ekängen outside Linköping to murder two boys their own age. They had most likely been told to do it by older criminals. According to some sources the boys were acquainted with each other, even friends.

The four of them had arranged to meet in Linköping, where they socialized, went to the movies, separated, then met later at an apartment they had access to.

That's where the plan was implemented. The older one got out his gun and shot one of the boys in the throat. He died immediately. Then he shot the other boy, a sixteen-year-old, several times, and one of the bullets went through his head. He also stabbed him repeatedly with a knife.

In spite of this, the boy survived.

Afterwards, the murderers took the train back to Malmö. They brought along the gun and the knife used in the attack, and when the train stopped in Helsingborg, an hour or so from Malmö, it was stormed by a number of police. In remand, the seventeen-year-old admitted that he'd shot and stabbed the boys. He claimed he did it in self-defence.

'Abbe is the murderer, Nick. Did you know that? The seventeen-year-old they're writing about is Abbe. He did it. But don't think about it, Nick. That thing he said about you letting him down. It's not your fault, okay? It's not your fault.'

71

Five months later Abbe was convicted of homicide and attempted homicide and sentenced to imprisonment in a youth correctional facility for three years and nine months.

That same day I was strolling down Bergsgatan with Amna and Rahim, who had just told me that his wife was pregnant.

Rahim seemed nervous. It was probably something to do with the pregnancy and that he would soon become a father, I thought. He said he was afraid of what it would mean for his children to be born into a family that the Malmö police – and many people in Malmö – associated with criminality and social damage. 'It's been haunting me my whole life,' said Rahim. 'I've tried to do justice to myself but it's always bitten me in the arse.'

We crossed Möllan Square. The street sweepers, with their rotating brushes which always make me think of the ice machines in skating rinks when they go round in circles, were polishing the cobblestones. I told him that this was his great asset, that he had a unique insight into Swedish society, and this was why he had saved so many lives.

'If Sweden understood who you are,' I said, 'and valued

your knowledge, your abilities, you'd have a ministerial post and a prize awarded to you by the King's own hand.'

Rahim laughed in his hoarse voice: 'Ha-ha, I'd really like to see that.'

We sat at one of Krua Thai's outside tables, eyeing our menus in silence.

The sun was hanging aslant over the rooftops on the other side of the square. I lowered the parasol until it surrounded us like a tent.

Something was eating at Rahim. It didn't have anything to do with the pregnancy. He had something that he wanted to tell me. He started rather hesitantly and seemed unsure whether to bring it up in front of Amna.

'Have you listened to that phone call to the emergency services?' he said. 'From the boy in Ekängen.'

'Yes,' I said. 'But it's unbearable listening to it.'

'What phone call?' asked Amna.

I explained that the sixteen-year-old boy who was shot by Abbe, but survived, had called the emergency services several times without being answered, only to be disbelieved once he was connected to an operator. The conversation was broadcast nationally on Sveriges Radio, and widely shared online. One can hear in the boy's voice how frightened he is of dying. One can hear how he passes out, how he pleads for help, saying that he's been shot in the head, stabbed several times, that his friend is lying dead right next to him, and that he is also going to die. But the woman at the emergency call centre doesn't believe him. She sounds snide and disinterested; she asks him how he can be talking to her if he's been shot in the head. It's horrific. I couldn't listen till the end. I felt that this conversation between a child who's just been shot in the head and stabbed, whose friend is lying dead next to him, and a member of the emergency staff whose duty and responsibility it is to help him, instruct him about what he needs to do to maximize his chances of surviving while waiting for the ambulance, *to believe him and trust in what he's saying*, but who instead does the opposite and treats him like a wrongdoer, attaching suspicion to him and quite literally abandoning him to die, is Sweden in a nutshell. Nothing that I have seen reflects more clearly the thoughtless indifference of how Sweden allows its children to die on the streets.

I railed. Kicked it up another notch, grew agitated and emotional.

Rahim looked down at his food.

The pot of curry stood untouched, with the cutlery still wrapped in a napkin.

'I have to tell you something, Nick,' he said after a while. 'And there's no easy way of saying it, so I'm just going to spit it out. That sixteen-year-old calling for an ambulance is Anja's son. Abbe tried to murder Anja's son that night in Ekängen. I wasn't sure I should tell you. But, you know, now I'm telling you anyway. Hey, don't let this fuck you up. Can you promise me that? Don't let it get you down. Hear what I say? Shake it off. Promise me, brother.'

* * *

We left the restaurant, crossed the square, then separated.

The evening was cool. People sat wrapped in blankets at outside tables under glowing heat lamps. They were talking and laughing. Even in my street, which was usually defined by its stillness, there were house parties and loud music.

I walked in, kept my jacket on, moved through the living room, where your camp bed was still leaning up against the wall, and went onto the balcony, where I sat down on a chair.

Darkness had fallen. The tall, leafy trees and the buildings were like black shadows against the lit-up sky. In the shoot-up park I could discern bodies in motion. And along the pavements, heavy as grape clusters, the lilac hung down, purple-glowing in the blackness.

I put my earpieces in. I went to the Sveriges Radio website. Found the telephone conversation. And pressed play.

SOS 112, what's happened?

Help me. I've been shot. Me and my friend.

What's your location?

I'm in Ekängen, just by the school here.

Ekängen? Were you shot in Ekängen?

Yeah, I'm shot in the head, in my neck, shoulder and hand.

What were you shot with?

What?

What were you shot with?

A pistol. Please come and help me.

Is your assailant still in your location?

No, they cleared out. Please come and help me, I'm dying.

But I don't understand, if you've been shot in the head, how come you're talking?

Never you fucking mind!

Excuse me?

Just come. Please just come.

Where did you say you were? Was it called Ekängen? By some school?

Yeah. Just come. I'm here. I'm bleeding to death.

But in Ekängen? I have to know where you are. Where exactly are you?

I'm lying here in the road. By the school. Outside the entrance.

What school is it? Ekängen School, is that what it's called?

Yes, please come.

Yes, we'll come once you tell me where you are.

Are you stupid or what? I'm by Ekängen School in Ekängen. By the entrance. Just come here.

Hello, you're going to have to pull yourself together. You want us to help you or what?

I'm going to die now. I'll die. Please come.

Yes, we are going to help you. What you said, then, was Ekängen, Ekängen School.

Yes, outside the school. By the entrance. Please come. I have a family.

Ekängen, you say. And outside a school there.

Please come.

Aha, is it Ekängen Academy?

Yes.

Not Ekängen School, but Ekängen Academy?

Yes. Please come.

A person here says he's been shot. In the head, the neck and the hand. (The emergency operator talks to a third party.)

And in the mouth and shoulder.

And in the mouth and shoulder.

Please come now.

What year were you born?

Beep

What's your telephone number?

Hurry.

Yes, yes, we've sent both police and ambulance.

When will they get here? I'll be dead in a few minutes.

What's your telephone number?

The number I'm calling from.

And what number are you calling from?

This one.

And what number is this one?

I can't take any more. I can't say it.

You can't say your number?

I can't talk. My mouth . . . my mouth is broken.

Okay, but can you say your telephone number?

Beep

Sorry?

Beep

Okay, great. Police and ambulance are on their way.

When will they be here?

Those who shot you, where are they now?

They left.

You know where they went?

No.

Where are you now exactly?

Outside the school on the ground.

Is that by the entrance?

Please come. I'm dying now.

We're coming, you'll see. They're on their way.

When will they be here?

I don't know. But they're on their way now, police and ambulance.

You have to tell my mother I love her. Tell my family I love them. Please say that.

Yes, yes.

Promise to say it.

Absolutely. But the shooting, did it happen just now or what?

Before I called. Just now.

Okay, so just now.

Yeah. I tried to call you before. I called you lots of times.

Absolutely.

And my friend here is dead. He's lying here next to me.

Excuse me?

My friend here is dead. I think he's dead. They shot him first.

Are you on your own or what?

My friend is lying here.

Okay. Those who shot you, do you know who they are?

No.

Okay.

Please can you come more quickly. I'm bleeding to death here.

Yes, they're on their way now.

Beep

I'm connecting you to the police now so you can talk to them.

(A dialogue between the police and the emergency operator follows.)

This is SOS Alarm. We have an ongoing case in Ekängen. By the school there. Ekängen Academy. The man is on the line, would you like to ask him anything?

Yes, please.

Very good, I'll connect him.

(The police are connected.)

Linköping police here.

When are you coming?

Who am I talking to?

When are you coming?

Pardon me, what did you say?

When will you be here?

When we're there?

Yes.

We're there in a moment. Who am I talking to?

Don't go on. Just come. Just come.

You're calling us. What's your name if you don't mind?

Are you stupid or what? He's shot me in the face. And stabbed me as well. I don't understand how I can be alive. Please come.

Who's been shot?

Me and my friend here. We're by the school. My friend is dead.

I understand. But do you have a name?

Beep I already told you.

You haven't at all. You haven't told me.

Beep

What's your surname?

Beep

Sorry?

Beep

And a telephone number.

I already gave it to you. Please just come now.

We're coming. But can you give me your telephone number?

Beep

I'm going to die. I'm going to die now. Please come.

We're coming. So you've been shot?

Yes.

With Elijah, a year before he moved in.

Photographed by Mikael Stiller for an exhibition, before Elijah moved in.

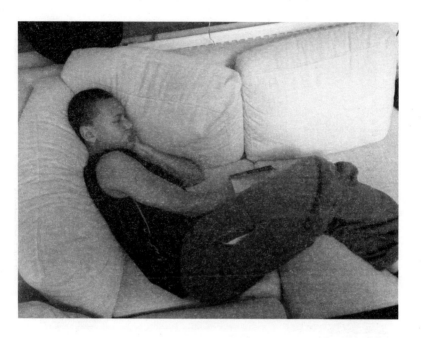

The first night in the apartment.

A haircut on Christmas Eve.

Snapshot of Elijah driving what's assumed to be a stolen car, aged fourteen.

Training with Elijah at the sports hall.

Elijah, aged fifteen, surrounded by books.

Elijah making his debut for the national youth team.

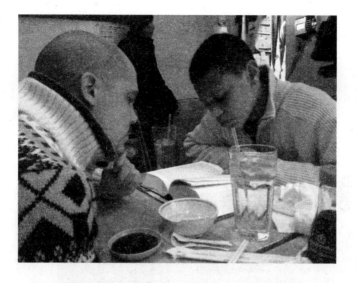

Reading Knausgård's *My Struggle* out loud in a sushi restaurant in Harlem.

At Holcombe Rucker Park, Harlem, New York.

On his birthday Elijah got 500 krona,
The Autobiography of Malcolm X and pancakes.

At the court near the apartment.
Bullet holes can be seen on the backboard.

Sources

p. 80 '**Poverty is not the worst . . . the wind or sun**': from Harry Martinson, *Nature: Poems* (Bonnier, 1934)

p. 99 '**Here we received the first blows . . . without anger**': from Primo Levi, *If This Is a Man*, translated from the Italian by Stuart Woolf (The Orion Press, 1959)

p. 126 '**No one should try to make poverty a thing of beauty . . .**': from Vilhelm Moberg, *When I Was a Child*, translated from the Swedish by Gustaf Lannestock (Knopf, 1956)

p. 128 '**First food, then ethics**': from Bertolt Brecht, *The Threepenny Opera*, 1928

p. 128 '**Streamers and placards can't be eaten**': from Cornelis Vreeswijk, 'Lullaby', *Ballads and Impertinencies*, 1964

p. 128 '**A hungry mob is an angry mob**': from Bob Marley, 'Them Belly Full (But We Hungry)', *Natty Dread*, 1974

SOURCES

p. 128 **'An empty belly leaves no room . . .'**: from George Orwell, 'As I Please', *Tribune*, 1943–7

p. 129 **'One asked Germans living . . . get the same answer'**: from Stig Dagerman, *German Autumn*, translated from the Swedish by Robin Fulton (Quartet Books, 1988)

p. 198 **'the higher up the street one came, the cheaper . . . shuffled about there'**: from Karl Ove Knausgård, *My Struggle 2: A Man in Love*, translated from the Norwegian by Don Bartlett (Vintage, 2013)

Nicolas Lunabba is one of the most influential voices in the Swedish debate regarding young people at risk of spiralling into violence and crime in neglected areas of the country, where gun violence is high. He runs Helamalmö, an organization committed to social justice, which aims to create a sense of safety and stability for the marginalized. In 2022, Lunabba was awarded the Swedish Martin Luther King prize for his work and received an honorary doctorate in social work from Malmö University.